Alaska Panhandle Tales

Or
Funny Things Happened Up North

By Jack O'Donnell

Copyright © by Jack O'Donnell

O'Donnell, Jack
  Alaska Panhandle tales / Jack O'Donnell.
  p. cm.
  LCCN: 95-83460
  ISBN 0-939116-40-5

  1. Alaska--History.   I. Title

F904.046 1996   979.8'2
                                    QBI96-20164

Published by Frontier Publishing
P.O. Box 441
Seaside, OR 97138

Printed in the United States of America

Table of Contents

Foreword

I want to dedicate this book to all the good people of FREE SPIRIT I have known in my lifetime in this great state of Alaska. All of them have contributed their bit in making it the last stronghold on this earth where one can still be an individual, where one can still do his own thing while respecting others, free from all the lemmings who seem to be inhabiting this world and forcing everyone to fit their mold. The names of individuals may have been changed at times to protect the guilty.

As for me, I think my very first attempt to

The author during his painting phase.

become an entrepreneur was when I was about five years old. My uncle had one of the very first automobiles in town. It was a Buick, about a 1920 Model of maroon color, of which he was very proud. The interior was immaculate. His son, my cousin Pat, and I were forbidden to even open the doors and enter this automobile, except when his dad invited us to do so. However, he had never specifically told us we could not repaint the outside of his pride and joy.

I had a bit of trouble convincing Pat it was the neighborly thing to do, but he finally agreed. There was a five-gallon bucket of roofing tar sitting nearby in the garage. No paint brushes were available, but we each located a stick we could dip into the tar and spread fairly evenly along the doors and hood. I painted on one side while my cousin did his painting on the opposite side. It went well until I heard an agonized scream as his father entered the garage and gave his son a good swat, that sent him bawling towards their home.

I had been so engrossed in painting, I had barely realized we had a visitor until I recognized the owner of the car, at which time I decided to depart also, but TOO LATE. He grabbed me by the collar as I went charging past for the door, and then swung my head around and down on their wood chopping block. With his other hand, he swung a double-bladed axe up high over my head and said, "Pray, you little bastard, cause where you're going you're going to need it." All I could do was look up at that axe which was about to descend and think, "Geeze, what a crank. We were only trying to upgrade your car!"

Obviously the axe didn't descend, or I wouldn't be writing this book, which I hope may give you a bit of chuckling now and then as you read on.

So to all the characters in this book, I say, in the Thlinget language, YAH-EEK-QUA-Sakeen, "so long."

About the Author

Jack O'Donnell was born in Alaska and has seen southeastern Alaska, known as the Panhandle, grow from an untamed land of individualists to the present-day almost too tame land of almost too subdued individualism.

His home is in Petersburg, the area where commercial fishing in season and guiding bear hunters when fishing was not in season has provided him a livelihood, a lot of fun, and some great stories.

In this book he lets you look in on what was often humorous — and always entertaining.— about early-day Alaska.

*Jack
O'Donnell*

A thank you to my daughters — Nancy, Diane, and Hazel — for all their help.

Part 1

Alaskans May Be a Little Different

Herman Papke

The Newcomers

Bob and Two Kamokes

"...the nurses gave him another bath. He protested that all his manhood scent was being removed and, from then on, nurses lacked any sex appeal for him...."

Herman Papke

Papke, as he was known to everyone in Petersburg, had arrived in Alaska working as a crewman on a small U.S. Coast and Geodetic Survey ship in 1907. They had spent most of their summer doing survey work in Wrangell Narrows, where Papke had observed a family of Indians living in a tiny shack on shore. Near the shack, was a fish smoking rack, where the Indians split and hung their salmon for both smoking and drying for winter food.

With survey work coming to an end, and the boat and crew soon departing, Papke elected to remain at Wrangell Narrows. As the Indians had lately departed with their winter's supply of fish, he had a ready-made cabin to move into. The survey boat and crew were only too happy to help him move his few belongings, plus a small amount of food ashore, before they departed.

Papke hurried before cold weather set in to get himself a winter's supply of fish. He rigged a hook on a long pole and used that to hook

Herman Papke

silver salmon that were attempting to leap up and over a small waterfall. The salmon could only ascend the waterfall during high tide when the water rose high enough to make it possible. Deer were plentiful and often one or more walked past within a few feet of the cabin. At that range, Papke could shoot a deer with an old .22 caliber rifle he had acquired from another crewman on the survey boat. An unlimited supply of crabs and clams were also available by merely wading along the shoreline at low tide.

The tiny cabin measured only ten feet by ten feet, with just enough room for an old homemade stove and a small bunk which was attached to one wall. This arrangement was ideal for Papke. The cabin was so tiny he could split wood to keep his stove hot without even getting out of bed. As for the floor, it was gravel and could be replaced by shoveling in another layer whenever it became too soiled from cooking and wood splitting. This was an ideal situation for one never noted for much ambition.

The first winter rolled by without too many problems, and when the Indians returned the following summer, they discovered their cabin already occupied. This forced them to construct another shelter for themselves a short way down the shore rather than risk an unpleasant scene with Papke. This tiny cabin, with only minor repairs now and then, was to be Papke's home for the next fifty years.

He managed to acquire a skiff and a net by fishing for Mountain Point Cannery which lay to the north of the cabin, about halfway to Petersburg. At the onset of World War I, Papke applied for U.S. citizenship and, fortunately, he was given credit for his work as a crewman on the survey ship. Otherwise, he undoubtly would have been interned for the duration of the war, as other German nationals were.

He had difficulty, however, selling his gillnetted silvers during this period of time, as the cannery tender often bypassed him in distaste of anyone of German descent. The salmon he was unable to sell, he utilized as fertilizer for his garden, which had to be expanded to accommodate the quantities of silver salmon he had to dispose of.

Once World War I ended, times improved for Papke, and by now his strawberries and raspberries were thriving, no doubt from all the rich fertilizer they had received. He would row into Petersburg occasionally, with his skiff overflowing with all kinds of produce, which he sold at the city float to customers anxious to buy fresh vegetables and berries.

The years went by and, eventually, a telephone line was strung from tree to tree from the end of the road at Mountain Point to Papke's, so he could telephone into Petersburg as the steamship from Seattle passed his cabin, to alert the dock manager of it's arrival in about one hour. Installing the telephone in Papke's tiny shack was a problem. By this time, he had accumulated a couple worn-out stoves, plus he always hung vegetables from his ceiling for drying. The only logical spot for the telephone was in his bunk, where he spent the majority of his days and nights anyhow. A space was cleared on the wall and the phone was attached.

This, of course, was long before today's modern telephones. It was necessary to crank the signal assigned to whomever you wished to converse with, using a small handle on the side of the phone case. As there were only a handful of telephones in Petersburg, everyone knew everyone else's signal. One short crank, then a longer crank, then another short crank signaled Dick Miller, the dock manager, that he had a message. When he answered, Papke would announce that the steamer had just passed his cabin northbound and was due in Petersburg in about an hour. This message was available on that same telephone line to anyone else who chose to eavesdrop.

This was probably the happiest period in Papke's life because, not only did he now have a telephone installed free just for him to announce the steamers arrival, but he also had access to anyone in town who had a telephone, and was unfortunate enough to have Papke discover their telephone signal. He could now lay in the bunk in his cabin and crank out signals to friends in town. These calls might come at one or two in the morning, or whenever Papke felt the urge to telephone them, for he always remained awake at night and slept all day. The unlucky person, who made the mistake of answering his signal, could only sit there and listen as Papke continued on and on about his problems with the robins, crows, ravens, or blue jays that were bothering his plants.

In 1935 the road was extended from Mountain Point to near Papke's cabin, making it possible for people to drive out and walk the shoreline over to Papke's for a visit with such a colorful character. It was fortunate that the road was now open and Papke had a telephone.

These links with town possibly gave him another lease on life.

Somehow, over the many years alone, he had survived with home remedies that he concocted when he became ill and, no doubt, some of these remedies actually helped keep him healthy. A pinch of some herb, plus a slice of onion, plus something else, all stirred together in a glass of warm water, with a little jigger of whiskey someone had given him as a gift, often made him feel better and lifted his spirits.

However, he foolishly tried one of his home remedies to soothe his hemorrhoids. He placed a chilled, pint-size bottle, small end first, up his rear end. This may have been something he had tried successfully before, but his luck ran out this time when, somehow, a vacuum formed and locked the pint bottle solidly in his rectum. No amount of twisting or turning on Papke's part could make it release. As time went on, it became very painful. I have no idea how long he had to endure this pain. Somehow he managed to ring town on his telephone, and advised them, "I have a bottle stuck in my ass and need help!"

Because Petersburg had no ambulance at this time, the local transfer truck was dispatched to drive down to Papke's shack and bring him back to the hospital. The transfer truck was a flatbed with no sides on it to keep the cargo, in this case Papke, from bouncing off on the rutted, gravel road.

On reaching the end of the road, the driver, Cliff Roundtree, parked the truck. He and his helper, Jake, took a 2 by 12 plank, long enough to carry Papke on, along the beach to his shack. They had no need to knock on his door, as he could be heard hollering in pain long before they got near.

They announced their arrival, and then got his door partially opened before it jammed against his wood chopping block. After rolling the chopping block aside, they finally got the door fully open. Because Papke was a very small person, the door was very tiny, less than two feet wide. Most people had to stoop almost double to enter the door.

Papke was laying in the bunk, facedown, which caused a bit of a problem. Somehow, they had to get him rotated onto their plank, then slide the plank with Papke attached out through the tiny door without causing him any additional pain. It was a struggle, but eventually they managed to get him outside.

Once outside, they set the plank down and took one of his blankets to throw over him for warmth and, for modesty's sake, to conceal the bottle which shone like a beacon out of his rear end. Even the weight of the blanket was painful to Papke, so they removed it. One walked ahead and one came behind carrying Papke face down on their makeshift stretcher. Papke hung on wildly to keep from rolling off onto the ground.

Once at the truck, they gently laid Papke

and the plank on the flatbed, and Cliff got into the driver's seat. It was necessary for Jake to ride in back and steady Papke, to prevent him from rolling off as they drove the pothole riddled road as carefully as possible. Each pothole in the road that the driver could not avoid, bounced the truck and brought howls of pain from Papke.

His howls could be heard far ahead, alerting people who rushed out of their homes to see what was creating the racket. All that could be seen was Reliable Transfer roaring past, with Jake holding a passenger steady who had something shiny sticking out of his rear end. This strange sight was a topic of conversation among the viewers, and curiosity ran wild until later in the day, when a more detailed account was available.

On his arrival at the hospital, Papke was rushed immediately to the operating room. The doctor punctured the base end of the bottle to allow air to rush in. This released the vacuum and the bottle. Papke was then given a thorough bath by the nurses, with him objecting loudly all the while.

He remained in the hospital overnight, and the next morning the nurses gave him another bath. He protested that all his manhood scent was being removed and, from then on, nurses lacked any sex appeal for him, due to their too frequent bathing. After breakfast and another examination by the doctor, Papke was released to happily wander down to main street and give his own account of his experience to anyone he could get to listen.

2

"The Indians loved music and, if General Custer had used his head, and had a violin or concertina with him at Little Big Horn, both Sitting Bull and Crazy Horse would have been dancing around him instead of removing his scalp!"

The Newcomers

Oscar Nicholson and Olaf Olson, cousins, shipped out on sailing ships from Norway, traveling eventually to San Francisco. There they both jumped ship and hired on as crewmen with Alaska Packers on one of their sailing ships that brought supplies and crews to their many canneries in Southeastern and Western Alaska. Arriving at Wrangell's cannery, they heard of a new cannery being built at the north end of Wrangell Narrows named Pacific Norway Packing Company. This cannery had Norwegian owners and nearly all Norwegian construction workers. The two cousins decided to quit their jobs again and managed to find transportation by small boat through Wrangell Narrows to the new settlement springing up near the cannery.

As both had been experienced net men in Norway, they immediately found work hanging and mending seines for the new plant. After working all day six days a week, they would hurry over to where they were building

Early Petersburg

themselves a cabin and work there until dark. Sundays they worked on their cabin all day.

Once the fishing season opened they were both placed in charge of a large, thirty-foot, flatbottom skiff, powered by oars. Two men sat side-by-side each pulling on his own oar. Two more men sat directly behind the first two, and pulled in time with them. No doubt this method of power was copied from the Roman galleys of old or, possibly, from the Vikings. It allowed these large seine skiffs to be propelled in shallow water where no motor-driven boats could possibly maneuver.

Only sockeye salmon were wanted for salting and canning because they retained their prized red flesh after being canned, or salted in barrels. Each sockeye stream usually had an Indian family living nearby who took sockeyes out of the stream to split and put on racks for drying and light smoking. The method they used to harvest their fish was to drive the salmon behind a fence of poles or rocks. Then when the tide receded and left the stream banks bare, they would hook out the stranded sockeyes.

It was necessary to negotiate with the chief of the family for permission to commence seining in salt water near the mouth of the stream to avoid arguments. Usually, if the male Indians were hired to help seine, it was okay. Oscar appeared to have the most diplomatic approach with the Indians, even though he spoke very little English himself as yet. He

Fishermen and construction crew, Petersburg Cannery, Circa 1900

seemed the most trustworthy to a race of people who had reason to have very little trust in the White Man's words. He always fulfilled his promises to the Indians and also saw that they received their wages at the end of the season.

Once the salmon season ended, the two cousins hurried to have a large skiff built so they too could enter the halibut fishery. For halibut fishing they would use different gear than the nets they had used for seining. They would use hooks and lines like they had used to fish cod in Norway. While they waited for their eighteen-foot skiff to be completed by a local carpenter, they rigged up groundline with hooks and gangions.

Once the skiff was finished and painted,

they launched it and gillnetted fresh herring for halibut bait, which was placed on their hooks by one cousin, while the other rowed them out to Frederick Sound to set the baited gear. They rowed ashore to walk the beach while allowing their gear to set on bottom for three hours, hoping to attract halibut to take their bait. Hauling their groundline back by hand was heavy work, but they were young and strong, plus anxious to make money.

Within a short time they were able to do as well as more experienced halibut fishermen. Once their gear had been hauled back into their boat, one would begin rowing the heavy skiff back towards Wrangell Narrows while the other dressed out their catch. They delivered the halibut at Scow Bay, three miles farther down Wrangell Narrows than the cannery settlement. Here on a large scow, the halibut were weighed, then iced with glacier ice which was available year-round from icebergs drifting ashore from Le Conte Glacier nearby.

A freight steamship stopped once weekly to load the iced and boxed halibut for shipment to Seattle, where it was sold at auction to local buyers. The fishermen received no money for their halibut deliveries until their halibut had been sold in Seattle and expenses for icing, boxing, and shipping had been deducted. If a large amount of halibut had arrived at the Seattle waterfront for auction on the same day, the price per pound might drop drastically due to a surplus. Other times, when only a small amount was placed on auction, the price might double for the day.

The two "Newcomers," as Olaf and Oscar were named by the others, continued to bait and fish their halibut gear each day that weather allowed them to row out into Frederick Sound to set and haul back their gear. Then began the long, slow row back past their cabin to Scow Bay to deliver their fish. They had to wait for fair tide to row to Scow Bay, and after unloading their halibut, they must also have fair tide for the return home. Usually they rowed home in the dark.

As the fall storms worsened, it was impossible to safely fish out of an open skiff for days on end. One by one the other competitors fishing halibut quit for the winter, to wait for the weather to improve in spring. Not the Newcomers, who seized every reasonably calm day to row out and set their gear in deeper and deeper water as winter progressed. Soon they were all alone and were the only skiff making halibut deliveries to Scow Bay.

Now it was midwinter and even the freight steamship had difficulty maintaining its schedule from Seattle due to winter storms. Often it was necessary to dump some of the halibut they had delivered to Scow Bay before the freight boat returned to load it, because it had been held too long and would not be in good condition when delivered in Seattle.

It was heartbreaking to have fish they had

worked so hard to catch, clean, and deliver be dumped overboard, and receive no payment for the many days of miserable, hard work. Still the two Newcomers kept on, determined to make some bit of earnings even in midwinter.

Shortly after Christmas, the freight boat returned from Seattle with payment for several deliveries the two cousins had made which had been delivered to Seattle and sold on the auction. Theirs had been the only fresh halibut available during the Christmas holidays, and the price had doubled due to the shortage. They received a payment of four hundred dollars which was a fabulous sum, even when divided two ways. Never again did the two cousins regret leaving Norway for the new country of America!

Now the days were short and the nights long. If it was stormy on the water, there was always need of firewood to keep their cabin warm. The muskegs directly behind the settlement had plenty of yellow cedar available that produced a hot fire, but burned quickly. The Indians all used this wood to heat their cabins, as most had no stove. The cabins had gravel floors, so an open fire could be kept burning safely all day at the center of the cabin. The small amount of wood smoke the yellow cedar produced drifted up and out through an opening in the roof.

The Indian men would tramp a trail in the snow out onto the muskeg, each following in the footsteps of the one ahead, until they reached the nearest available yellow cedar trees. Here they would stop to chop down each cedar tree with an axe. Then they peeled the bark from the tree just as one peels a banana. Once the bark was removed, they would again drive their axe blade into the front end of this peeled log and commence dragging it back downhill in their packed-down footsteps. The log would slide easily due to the greasy surface of the peeled log.

After a few trips had been made downhill from the muskeg, towing a yellow cedar log by its tapered end, this trail would become glazed ice like a toboggan slide. Then it was only necessary to fall the tree, chop it into twenty-foot lengths and place it in the log slide. Then, a good push from behind would start it on its run, unaided, all the way to the trail's end at the settlement. Each Indian would put his own distinguishing mark on each of his logs with his axe, so he could retrieve his own at the trail's end when he returned to the settlement at dusk.

Occasionally some of the white men from the settlement would also tramp up through the snow pulling a Yukon sled which they would load with yellow cedar logs for the trip downhill. The Yukon sled is similar to a regular dogsled but has no handlebars and no brake. It can carry a mighty load of logs if stacked correctly. *Beware* though of driving your double-bladed axe into the log stack for the trip downhill!

Many men did this. Then to get the sled started downhill they had to move to the front of the sled and start pulling on it. Once the sled got started, it picked up momentum like a runaway train, but this runaway had razor-sharp axe blades sticking out of it. Soon the pullers were being overtaken by the sled. They had visions of those axe blades performing a sex change operation immediately, unless they dove out of the sled's path as it swished by!

Most white men preferred to saw spruce logs into firewood, because spruce burned longer than cedar in their stoves. They would fall a large spruce tree along the shoreline and float it clear of the shore at high water. Then they would tow it to a spot near their cabins and allow it to settle down as the tide receded. This made it convenient for sawing into wood blocks.

When the weather was too miserable even for wood cutting, often the men would play cards in one of the larger cabins. Usually someone had made a batch of homebrew or some wine fermented from raisins. Those with musical talent would bring out their accordions and violins. The Indians would all come and stand outside the cabin where the music was being played, even in the worst weather. The Indians loved music and, if General Custer had used his head, and had a violin or concertina with him at Little Big Horn, both Sitting Bull and Crazy Horse would have been dancing around him instead of removing his scalp!

If the musicians could harmonize together well enough for a Swedish Waltz, or Scow Bay Waltz, as it was know locally, some of the Indian maidens would be invited inside to dance with the white men. Perhaps the maidens would be offered a drink of wine to overcome their aloofness toward the Norwegian Codfish Eaters! If the wine worked its wonders, they might also be danced right out the back door and over to the dancer's cabin during intermission.

All in all this time of short days and long nights was a pleasant break before the rush of the salmon season began again. During salmon season everyone worked around the clock, for it was daylight most of the time.

The Newcomer, Oscar Nicholson, recognized early on that this cannery settlement, eventually named Petersburg after its founder Peter Buschman, was situated in one of the most productive areas in Alaska, and was destined to become an important seaport for many new industries springing up as the years went by. He started the first movie theater of one reel movies, which he later sold when he became superintendent of Petersburg Packing Company which absorbed Pacific Norway Packing Company, where he and his cousin had begun hanging nets when they first arrived. He was a trusted manager who worked up from the very bottom of the heap to a position of importance in the newly-founded townsite.

3

"Bob had an air horn connected to the surplus air going to the carburetor and this he used every few yards to warn pedestrians he was approaching."

Bob and Two Kamokes

B ob Kechison had landed in Petersburg after spending some time in Nome dealing cards in Tex Rickard's card room during the Nome gold rush. Tex Rickard later became Jack Dempsey's manager. When the gold rush collapsed, Bob drifted from town to town, finally settling in Petersburg where he opened the Arctic Card Room.

He had one wooden leg and walked with a cane. He had a dog he named Kamoke (a term used in Panguinge card games). His dog was his inseparable companion, and laid at his feet when he was dealing cards. Bob attended Enge's theater when each new movie was shown, and Kamoke also attended, sitting beside Bob, attentively watching the movie. As a kid, I would often sit beside Kamoke at the movie, because Bob shared a Hershey bar with Kamoke and would also share part with me.

When Prohibition came to an end in 1933, Bob had neither the finances nor the desire to reopen his card room as a bar. Once liquor was

Bob Kechison

available at the other card rooms his business collapsed to zero, and he soon closed up and retired. After his retirement, he bought a used Chevrolet, about ten years old, with a four cylinder engine which he drove around the few streets of Petersburg. He gave many of us kids a ride in the rear seat, provided we remained quiet like Kamoke, who sat beside Bob in the front seat with no other rider allowed up there. Bob had an air horn connected to the surplus air going to the carburetor and this he used every few yards to warn pedestrians he was approaching. This was a wise move, for he had never driven a car before, and it took sometime for him to learn to coordinate both the steering wheel and the various pedals with only one usable foot. I think Bob endured us kids riding along in his car because we each took turns cranking to get it started, as it had no self-starter.

Kamoke was now nearly twelve years old and needed help to climb up onto his front seat station in the car. It was apparent that he too, like his master, was not in the best of health any longer. He was becoming more and more reluctant to even get excited about cruising around town in their "tooting" automobile. There was very little road anyway except in town. The gravel road out to Scow Bay and beyond terminated at the old Mountain Point Cannery site and was not well maintained. Bob never risked driving farther than Scow Bay.

When the first snow arrived each year, his car was placed in a shed until the following May. During the winter of 1933, Kamoke reached the point where he was unable to even get to his feet, and Bob had to have him put to sleep. Bob was a quiet man, but it was obvious he grieved deeply for his faithful companion who had weathered so many experiences with him.

Friends encouraged him to get another dog for a companion, but he would just shake his head. However, when spring arrived and it was again time to get his automobile out, Bob found himself a new pup and, of course, named him Kamoke. This new Kamoke delighted in sitting up front with Bob, and it was obvious he was winning over some of the deep affection Bob had held for his first Kamoke. However, Bob had managed during his years in the card room to silence his old friend from barking when someone entered his establishment. After Bob retired from the card room and furnished a small cabin for himself nearby, perhaps Kamoke had become so deaf through old age he never bothered to bark when someone came to visit them.

Not so, though, with the new Kamoke. He barked up a storm when anyone walked past on the road or knocked at their door to visit, and this troubled Bob a lot. I stopped to visit with him nearly every day, and spent much of the visit petting the young Kamoke, who seemed to like me too. Bob noticed this and mentioned that, if I wished, he would give his new friend to me. He said the constant barking was too much for him. I was, of course, absolutely delighted to become Kamoke's new master, but it took some persuasion to get my parents to allow it. They went personally to Bob to discuss his reasons for offering me his pet. They finally gave their consent, and from that day on, Kamoke went everywhere I went, except to school.

Part 2

Business As Usual—and Not So Usual

4   *"...it was illegal to have liquor in your possession. However, Mr. Wheeler could sell a laxative that contained enough alcohol to make one feel it."*

Wheeler Drug and Jewelry

Wheeler Drug and Jewelry was the only drugstore in Petersburg for many years. It had all the newspapers from Seattle which arrived by steamer once a week. When I was about seven or eight, I began selling papers for Mr. Wheeler, the owner. The first few times I was paid with a candy bar or a roll of Lifesaver mints. About the third time I returned to his store with the money I had received for selling even old, old *Washington Postens,* a Norwegian Language paper, plus week old Seattle newspapers, my Mexican-Indian friend, Johnny Adams, came with me. He was a competitor and sold papers also, but he told me I was being robbed as I should be getting five cents per paper instead of a nickel candy bar for all of them. When Mr. Wheeler again went to pay me off with one candy bar after selling my entire ten newspapers, Johnny exploded and demanded that I be paid the same commission as the others. Mr. Wheeler did not argue with my lawyer, but handed over my fifty cents which, of course, I spent buying candy in his store.

We kids were not old enough to buy cigarettes, as most of the other paper sellers were about seven or eight years old also. However, Harold and Johnny Holten, twins our age, could enter Mr. Wheeler's and buy Cubeb cigarettes for their asthma. Apparently it was believed this would clear up the congestion in their chests. The smoke from these Cubebs smelled awful to any passer-by, and they tasted almost as bad. However, we all developed hacking coughs immediately, just like the Holten twins, and spent our paper money on Cubebs, which Mr. Wheeler was pleased to sell to all of us at exorbitant prices. God, what a smoke screen we would lay down when we all lit up our Cubebs at one time.

I never saw Mr. Wheeler when he was not dressed in a white shirt and necktie plus his black hat. Even when out in front of his store chopping ice or snow clear of the door, he was always dressed to the hilt.

There were two huge glass balls that hung in the store windows. One red and the other green, and the lights reflected off them making it seem a bit cheery, looking into the store. I suppose he had a pharmacist license himself, but he always had a red-headed female clerk who possibly was the pharmacist. Over the years the clerks came and went, but all of them were redheads. I know whenever people fell ill or thought they had a cold coming on, they could stop at Wheeler Drug Store and Mr. Wheeler would sell them either some medicine off the shelf or, if he had none, he would mix up something himself for them to take home and use. This would be unthinkable nowadays with rigid professionalism and boundaries between a doctor and pharmacist.

Wheeler's calendar each year was like an almanac as it showed the time of sunrise and sunset each day. I would check it religiously each day after December twenty-second to see how much daylight was gained.

This was in the 1920s during Prohibition when it was illegal to have liquor in your possession. However, Mr. Wheeler could sell a laxative that contained enough alcohol to make one feel it. I remember the bottles had a sketch of a Monk holding a basket of grapes, which apparently made the elixir a medication for the ill. I think Mr. Wheeler limited purchase of the elixir to one bottle per customer per visit. Naturally, some of the more seriously ill would return frequently for an additional bottle. I believe the Prohibition authorities frowned on this activity and eventually got it stopped.

The same thing happened with raisins that sold at the grocery store in about five pound cartons with a warning inside that under no circumstances should one ever put these raisins in a container of water and add sugar, as it would cause fermentation which, in approximately one week, would become an illegal substance with over 3.2 percent alcohol content (the maximum allowable legal content). This created a rush to the grocery store to purchase cartons of raisins for pies and bread making by half the townspeople.

It all goes to show our Yankee Ingenuity when put to a real test!

5

"...they all waited for him to be returned so he could be worked over good. But the stool pigeon had wisely insisted on a paid steamship ticket out of Ketchikan in exchange for his testimony."

Prohibition Afloat and Ashore

Prohibition of liquor went into effect January 1, 1918, as the Eighteenth Amendment. Passed by Congress and called the Volstead Act, it was probably the most unpopular amendment ever passed, and probably, the only reason it did pass, was because a majority of the public did not bother to vote. Once it took effect, people who never cared a hoot about consuming liquor immediately decided no one could tell them what they could or could not consume in the privacy of their homes.

Illegal liquor immediately became popular with all but a handful of "Blue Noses," as they were scoffishly called, who demanded that prohibition laws be enforced. A whole new set of bureaucrats were appointed to enforce the law, and were called "Prohis" by the public.

There were liquor stores in most towns in the U.S.A., including Alaska, which had to sell out their supply of liquor before midnight New Year's Eve, 1918. Frank James drove taxi in Ketchikan, Alaska, and the last day liquor was legal, he was kept busy driving customers to and from the liquor store, some with cases of liquor they intended to stash away and use as they wished.

As midnight approached, the Ketchikan liquor store lowered prices on all remaining stock by twenty-five percent. This brought on another rush to the liquor store for bargain hunting. Several of Frank's customers inquired if he had stocked up on booze for the future, but he said, "Naw. I don't drink the damned stuff anyway so why buy it?"

At eleven p.m. the liquor store dropped its prices on all remaining liquor by fifty percent. When Frank heard this, he thought perhaps it would be wise to buy a case to give away the following Christmas as gifts for his friends. He bought a case of what remained for sale, which was actually some of the poorest liquor and had been passed up by even the local alcoholics as "rotgut". Frank loaded his case of rotgut into his taxi and took it home to slide under his bed until the following Christmas.

Half a year later on July fourth, he picked up a passenger from a halibut schooner at the city float. The passenger inquired if Frank knew anywhere in Ketchikan that a person might buy a bottle of whiskey to celebrate the Fourth of July. "Right off-hand I don't," said Frank. "I'd pay twenty dollars for a quart of good whiskey," his passenger lamented. "Why don't you just wait here," Frank said, "I just thought of someone who might have a bottle to sell." Unloading his passenger at one of the card rooms, Frank turned around, drove home, picked up a quart of his liquor, and returned to sell it for twenty dollars, ten times what it had cost him New Year's Eve.

Not long after on that same day, another halibut fisherman approached him and inquired if he might be able to locate another quart for him for the same price. "Wait here and I'll be back," Frank advised him, then took off again back home for another quart to dispose of at one thousand percent profit.

Before July fourth was over, he had sold the entire case at the same profit. This set him to thinking, "If these damned fools will pay me ten times what whiskey is worth, I might as well make it a business."

No liquor was available in Ketchikan, of course, but Prince Rupert, British Columbia, lay only ninety miles to the south and had no silly prohibition laws like the U.S. Liquor was available by the boatload if one had the money to spend. Also a majority of fresh halibut was sold and unloaded there by American boats for transshipment by rail back east. What easier way to have liquor delivered in Ketchikan, U.S.A., than by paying a friendly halibut captain to buy liquor with your money, load it aboard his boat after dark, and return to Ketchikan as a legitimate halibut boat innocent of any type of illegality. It was necessary, of course, to pay the captain a good margin of profit for the risk of being caught with illegal liquor.

At the beginning this worked great, but before long some of the loudmouthed fisherman had talked too much and the Revenue Cutters began a practice of stopping and searching many of the empty halibut boats returning home from Prince Rupert, looking for contraband liquor.

Every guilty halibut boat captain caught with illegal liquor insisted it was for his own consumption, bought legally with the intention of throwing any excess overboard before arriving in Ketchikan. The Revenue Service would listen to none of this. All liquor was confiscated and the halibut boat was towed into Ketchikan for a trial. Usually the fine served to the halibut captain was not too severe, but his days of smuggling liquor were over. From then on this particular boat was stopped whenever returning from Prince Rupert and searched with a fine tooth comb.

Soon it became difficult to find any halibut captain that would run the risk of transporting liquor into U.S. waters. Those that would insisted on delivering their cases of liquor to another American boat, that must meet them well within Canadian waters and off-load the liquor. The second boat then assumed the risk of being caught. Still plenty of illegal liquor managed to slip past the Revenue Cutters who may have felt a bit of sympathy at times for someone returning with liquor legal in one town but illegal in another.

The prohibition agents had their hands full

in the towns as well as on the water. They pulled surprise searches 'on any place suspected of having liquor to sell on the premises. Usually, any place selling liquor by the drink kept only one bottle on the premises. This bottle could quickly be smashed into the sink or the contents flushed down the toilet.

Frank had entered the liquor business too, but sold only by the quart to customers he knew and felt safe accepting money from. He kept his supply of liquor from Prince Rupert cashed behind his home. Individual bottles were removed from the cases and placed under stumps. It would be difficult for any Prohis to snoop around without being seen by either Frank or some of his relatives living nearby. This worked well for almost a year, but the Prohis knew Frank was in the illegal liquor business, and were determined to catch him in the act of delivering to a customer.

The jails were full of prisoners who had been caught for selling illegal liquor, but getting one bootlegger to inform on another was nearly impossible. Finally, one was offered a shortened sentence if he would testify in court that he had purchased liquor from Frank. Because Frank considered him a friend, the Prohis planned a setup whereby Frank could be caught in the act of delivering liquor for resale to this party.

At this same time, the Revenue Cutter was in the shipyard a short two blocks from Frank's home. The Cutter agents were alerted to prepare for a liquor arrest, and to have their searchlights ready to beam directly at Frank's house.

The stool pigeon drove out in a cab to Frank's, and waited in the cab while Frank went out behind his house to get two quarts of liquor for the sale. Allowing what he considered time enough for Frank to be returning with the liquor, he had the taxi driver flip his lights on and off twice to signal Frank that all was well. Instead all Hell broke loose as the Cutter's searchlight caught Frank strolling down a path from his liquor hideout with a quart in each hand. Silhouetted in the bright light, Frank froze as Prohis agents erupted from both sides of his property and arrested him.

At his trial, the stool pigeon testified he was waiting with cash to purchase the liquor. Frank admitted he had no alibi. The judge before sentencing demanded that both bottles of liquor be opened so he would know for certain that each contained illegal liquor. When this was done, the judge poured himself a drink from each bottle to satisfy himself that both were actually good Scotch liquor. Setting both bottles back behind his desk, he delivered a sentence of six months to Frank to be served in the Ketchikan Jail.

Wishing to get his jail time over as soon as possible, Frank opted to begin his sentence immediately and was escorted to the jail to begin serving time. Once the other prisoners heard who had testified against Frank, they all waited for him to be returned so he could be worked over good. But the stool pigeon had wisely insisted on a paid steamship ticket out of Ketchikan in exchange for his testimony.

The jail time was more or less harmonious, because the jail was filled with bootleggers who were all Ketchikan locals and knew one another. Each prisoner was assigned a job; cooking, dishwashing, mopping floors, washing clothes, etc. When free of work, they joined in card games in progress.

All confiscated liquor was stacked in a barred enclosure at the jail. The enclosure was chained and padlocked and was only opened when more confiscated liquor arrived to be stored. Frank noticed immediately that the two quarts opened by the judge and tasted by him for Frank's conviction, had not arrived for storage, nor did they ever arrive during his six months sentence. This made him boil, naturally, as he was certain the judge had taken this evidence home for his own pleasure, the son-of-a-bitch.

Also, at various times, the guards came in with the key, open the door, unlock the chain, enter the liquor room, remove two or more quarts from a case, then relock the door and chain and depart with the liquor. This set the prisoners to discussing the disgraceful situation of being imprisoned for possessing liquor, while the dirty bastards who were hired to guard them were drinking the very liquor they had been imprisoned for possessing.

They discussed the prospects of breaking into the liquor storage themselves without the guards discovering it. Frank noticed that, though the door was padlocked as well as chained, the other side of the door was hinged with removable bolts. Working quietly when the guards were not present, it wasn't long before the group had the pins pulled. One prisoner slipped through the opening, grabbed two quarts of liquor, and slipped back into the jail room, while others returned the pins to the hinges and returned to their card table. Now, whenever the guards would leave the room, a bottle of whiskey was passed around to be shared by all.

Frank never drank liquor so passed his turn, but began thinking about the prospects of getting even with the son-of-a-bitch hypocrites who would take the confiscated liquor home for their own consumption. As a local man with property, he was allowed to be escorted to the local barber shop once a month for a haircut. Usually, while he waited his turn for a haircut, the guard would go next door for a cup of coffee and a piece of pie.

At his next monthly trip to the barber shop, Frank wore his topcoat as no prison garb was ever issued to prisoners. Under the topcoat, he had slipped a quart of whiskey into each leg of his pants to be held up by his hands in his pockets. As usual, his guard went next door to drink coffee and flirt with the waitress. During the guard's absence, Frank slipped the two quarts of booze to the barber and received forty dollars in exchange.

Sadly, however, all good things sooner or later come to an end. Not all the prisoners could handle all this free liquor. Some got drunk and one pissed in one of the guard's empty boots rather than wait his turn for the bathroom. This caused an eruption, and though no bootlegger would squeal on another, the guards shortly had another chain strapped tightly around the hinges and padlocked to make entry impossible without the proper keys.

6

"The Norwegian would really begin to fly in full volume as she gave Mr. Enge hell for failure to keep the movies showing correctly."

The Variety Theater and Rasmus

People with an education were held in awe when I was a kid. Very few people had ever progressed to the eighth grade, and most had not even reached that before they were needed at home to help with chores.

Many people in business had difficulty ordering more supplies, so traveling salesmen came through the town regularly, checking the shelves for the store operators and filling out the orders that their particular company stocked. Each brand of coffee, baking powder, salt, etc. had its own salesman as did many hardware supplies. Still, now and then an emergency would arise when a business man would need a letter written immediately to refill some depleted item. Most often anyone holding even a high school diploma was requested to write a letter for the owner.

Such a man was Tex. He was a loner, drifter, who had stopped off in Petersburg mostly because he only had steamboat fare for that port from Seattle. To make ends meet he had taken a job delivering telegrams around town. Telegrams were our only means of fast communication in early days, transmitted from town to town by the "Dot-Dot-Dot" of Morse Code and operated by the U. S. Army Signal Corps. Tex received fifty cents for each telegram he delivered, but barely delivered enough daily to feed himself. To supplement his income, he also typed out business letters at so much per word.

Rasmus Enge (pronounced "eng-gee"), who owned and operated the Variety Theater, often called him over to make out a business letter for him. Mr. Enge was a Norwegian immigrant who, although doing well in business in Alaska, had barely mastered the language. He would thus begin his dictation with Tex, "Paramount Pictures, Hollywood, California. Send me films, you dirty bastards! Signed Rasmus Enge." Tex would, of course, delete the worst words and use more discreet language instead.

Mrs. Enge did all the ticket selling at the Variety Theater plus the sweeping and cleaning each day before show time. There was only one showing per night so everyone made certain to be there early. Mr. Enge would fill the wood furnace completely with wood before making his final round checking the steam radiators which often became air locked due to low water pressure. Enge would give each a big wallop with a hammer to displace any air lodged in the pipes, as it was essential in winter to have some heat coming out of the four radiators, two on each side of the theater about thirty feet apart.

The theater was sitting on piling over the tide flats with no insulation whatever on the floors or walls so, naturally, everyone tried to find a seat as near as possible to a gurgling radiator. Those unfortunates who had to sit out in the middle of the theater had better have come heavily dressed and plan on moving their feet constantly on the cold, cold floor to maintain circulation.

Rasmus and Mrs. Enge

This was the only theater in town, and we had no radios or television in Southeastern Alaska, so it was an event just to come to the theater and see a movie. Each movie would continue to run every night for a week or more until the next batch of film arrived by the weekly steamer. The local advertising slides were always shown first for several minutes with no sound, of course, as there was no sound for the films until around 1930 in Petersburg. Next came the news that had been filmed months before but Mary Allen, the local spinster, would now begin playing the piano down in the orchestra pit at the lower front of the stage. For each news clip that was shown, Mary Allen would play her interpretation of what type of music was appropriate.

If the clip was of people walking the city streets somewhere, she played lightly tinkle, tinkle, tinkle music, but when a Navy news scene was shown of battleships steaming across the ocean with flags flying, her music would become loud with heavy hammering on the bass chords as she came down heavy on the piano keys. This necessitated bouncing six inches up and down away from her piano stool for each crescendo. Only miraculous balance, plus a reed-thin physique, allowed her to return each time to her piano stool.

Once the battleship faded from the scene, we would next see a silent Calvin Coolidge donning an Indian feather headdress or perhaps being presented with a ten gallon hat by a group of Texas oil men. This, of course, meant Mary Allen reverted back to light tinkle, tinkle music, leaving her piano stool only a few inches each raffling, and returning squarely to exact center each time. Marvelous!

Once the news was finished, the main event would begin. Often it was a Western, which everyone loved, as they were exciting and everyone had their favorite cowboy actor; Tom Mix, Buck Jones, Yakima Canutt, William Farnum, and a host of others. There was always a bunch of crooks, who wore black Stetsons so we could know they were the crooks. They all wore several day's growth of beard, and would leer and scowl into the camera. There was also a helpless maiden who had been abducted from her father's ranch by the crooks, and was held hostage while the crooks rustled her father's cattle to drive across the border into Mexico to sell.

The good guys always wore cream colored Stetsons, and their horses could always outrun the crooks' horses. The good guys would always manage to gain on and overtake the crooks, who by now, were emptying their revolvers over their shoulders, firing at least a dozen shots without reloading or even hitting a horse. Oh yes! Usually about this time several hundred Indians would also enter the chase, firing arrows indiscriminately at both good guys and bad guys who had wandered onto Indian land. Neither were welcome.

Now the good guys would gallop their horses down into a ravine and disappear completely while they rounded up their stolen cattle and turned back with them towards the ranch, after liberating the heroine, of course. She had been left dangling over a cliff while the hero and the leader of the bad guys fought back and forth with their fists. Eventually, the hero knocked the bad guy off the cliff and retrieved the heroine, who sometimes gave him a hug but never a kiss. That was too soppy. Meanwhile the Indians and bad guys were still racing across the prairies mixing it up with arrows and flying lead.

Mary Allen was trying to keep her music in pace with the events as they happened, which wasn't easy. No wonder she never gained an ounce. She knocked herself out every evening, except Sunday, hammering away on the piano, leaping from her stool ten times a minute at times as the situation warranted. It seemed the movies were not the same on Sunday without Mary Allen present at the piano keeping pace with things. The same exciting movie became just "ho hum" without her accompaniment.

However, there was usually someone like Lola King in the audience, who got carried away with the events going on up on the screen and began shouting out "Shoot him, Goddamit, before he shoots you in the back, for Christ's sake!" Someone nearby in the theater would then shout out, "Shut up, Lola, Goddamit, and just watch the movie!"

Often some smart aleck would sneak up to the projection room with a bottle of liquor to visit Mr. Enge, who operated the movie projector. He enjoyed his liquor, but Mrs. Enge tried desperately to prevent him from getting any, as he would immediately show the effects from one or more drinks. It would soon become noticeable to the audience, as the advertising slides of local businesses would begin to appear upside down as often as right side up. There would be an occasional whistle from some crank in the audience to show their displeasure, but most of the audience would remain silent hoping the erratic upside down advertising was merely a mistake and the show could begin shortly.

Next would come a short Mack Sennett comedy. There would be an abrupt break in action between reels sometimes, if Mr. Enge neglected to get the adjoining reel prepared for showing. This would plunge the theater into total darkness until the next reel eventually began and lit up the screen, and the audience could once again see who sat beside and in front of them.

If this happened more than once, the audience would begin to mutter louder, and several would stamp their feet in displeasure. Mrs. Enge who had been selling tickets at the entrance, and had been oblivious till now that something was wrong, would start up the stair steps to the projection room muttering to herself in Norwegian.

The Norwegian would really begin to fly in full volume as she gave Mr. Enge hell for failure to keep the movies showing correctly. If she also found someone with him who had given him liquor, the guilty person would receive her loudest condemnations, as they scurried to escape the flashlight that she carried to find her way in the dark.

By now, of course, the theater was in total darkness for Mr. Enge would let the reel run out as he defended himself, also in Norwegian. The audience joined in the argument by stamping their feet and whistling until the entire theater was in complete bedlam.

Finally, after shouting and arguing with Mrs. Enge, Mr. Enge made his escape down the stairs, throwing on the lights as he departed so the audience could see to leave as well. He took off for home, leaving her to walk to the front of the theater, climb the stairs and wave her flashlight for the audience's attention, and sadly inform everyone, "No show tonight. Enge is drunk." Then she would come back down the steps, and walk back up the aisle to the theater entrance, to hand each departing person a return ticket for the next night's show.

Most of the audience was rather resigned to this part of going to the theater, as it happened occasionally when some jackass managed to sneak past Mrs. Enge's vigil and offer liquor to Mr. Enge. Some in the audience, that were new to Petersburg, thought if they showed enough displeasure the movie might commence. They were left sitting stunned and alone as the regulars hastened to the entrance of the theater to get their return stub and get outside.

There they would wait, and listen to the torrent of Norwegian shouting that began once Mrs. Enge could lock the doors to the theater and focus her attention on Mr. Enge, who was lurking in the dark across the street where their home was located. If he dared shout across the street in reply, another storm of Norwegian was directed at him immediately.

Despite these occasional loud outbursts, Mrs. Enge often mentioned to her close friends, "Yes, I really kind of love the little devil."

7

"The men's toilet was merely a large opening in the floor with a low bulkhead to prevent anyone from dropping through to the beach twenty or more feet below. It created a dizzying effect for anyone unfortunate enough to really have to go."

Johnny Sales and His Pile Driver

Johnny Sales was a fine old gentleman from South Carolina who spent a good share of his later life in Petersburg. He loved the taste of whiskey and moonshine and would pour himself half a glass from a demijohn he always kept handy under his sink. The demijohn was unmistakable, as it was clothed in bamboo to avoid breakage.

He was a frustrated farmer, displaced in Alaska. He always had a few pigs rooting around on the hillside whenever the ground was clear of snow. People always chuckled at his efforts to create a farm, but he had the last laugh, as the pigs eventually cleaned away all the forest of tree stumps that had discouraged others from buying the land.

Over the years he built several shacks in Petersburg. However, what decided him to build a dance hall and soft drink parlor way out on the outskirts of town was a mystery, for there were probably only a dozen cars in town, at most. Prohibition of liquor was in effect, so there was no possibility of earning a profit selling liquor. Besides, he always offered his guests a free drink, so apparently had no plans for a Speakeasy.

He spent years struggling alone to get his dance hall constructed. When finally completed it was barely adequate to stop the rain from dripping in. He had an outhouse for women at one end of the hall, and another for men at the other end. The men's toilet was merely a large opening in the floor with a low bulkhead to prevent anyone from walking right in and dropping through to the beach twenty or more feet below. It created a dizzying effect for anyone unfortunate enough to really have to go. When the tide was high, the distance down was not as far, of course, but then there was always the danger of drowning. Most men familiar with his toilet facilities used to slip out the back door exit and relieve themselves on the dance hall wall.

Needless to say, there was very little profit for Johnny, as half the customers entered through the back door to avoid the admission fee. Actually, I think Johnny really didn't care, as he was more interested in having company and enjoyed visiting with everyone. He invited his special friends back to his living quarters in the rear, where he always poured everyone a free drink of his moonshine.

His main source of income was his pile driver which was constructed on a scow with a log A-frame to accommodate the hammer

Pile Driver

which weighed perhaps three hundred pounds. A piling was hoisted up to the maximum height of the A-frame, perhaps forty feet, then sharpened on the bottom end with an axe to allow it to drive downward into the mud flats. This piling would then be lowered until the end touched bottom, which usually was ten feet or less. This was to make certain the piling, when driven as deeply as possible, would still have at least ten feet remaining above water at high tide.

Each time the hammer was hoisted to its maximum height on the A-frame tracks, the front end of the scow would dip deeper into the water, as the one-cylinder engine labored to pull the hammer. Then, when the hammer was released to drop and hit the top of the piling, the engine would run freely, "Putt-putt-putt," and the front of the scow would leap upward creating a rocking horse effect. Then again, "Putt-putt-putt," as the engine struggled once more to lift the hammer skyward. Everything would, of course, be creaking and groaning and laboring as the hammer continued to rise and fall.

If a piling could be driven four feet down into the mud, Johnny considered that sufficient, and the driving ceased. Far too often, the lifting pressure of the tidewater at extreme high tide, plus a slight bump from a boat making a poor landing, was enough to have some of Johnny's driven pilings leap out of the mud, unless they had been fastened securely to another structure.

Johnny always seemed to take it all pleasantly and, if necessary, would return and redrive the same piling a second time. He owned the only pile driver available, so people who needed repairs done, or needed a new dock constructed, couldn't get too sarcastic about his pile driving, or they might wait years for him to return again.

He never married while in Petersburg and, if he did enjoy a secret love life with any woman in town, he kept it very discreet over the years.

Once his pigs had cleared enough ground for Johnny to plant a vegetable garden, he fenced-off that area and had truckloads of shrimp shells unloaded. He then shoveled the shells into a wheelbarrow and spread them all over the ground. The shells soon decayed and the stench was so nauseating people nearly choked walking past. Cars would roll up their windows and floor the throttle to escape the odor as quickly as possible. Pedestrians were not so fortunate, and had to stagger on past without drawing a breath as long as possible.

His garden flourished each season, and the neighborhood continued to endure the stench, partly because he was such a pleasant man, and partly because he always gave away most of his crop to anyone who stopped to visit.

He was generous to all and was always a happy man.

8 *"Now came the upstart White Man who decided he was to be the new King of Admiralty. Obviously these three bear hadn't heard about the White Man king and still considered themselves boss...."*

Bears and Fox Farming Don't Mix

Immediately after graduating from Petersburg High School, I accepted the opportunity of working at a fox farm on Dorn Island in Seymour Canal. Seymour Canal is not actually a canal, but at its extreme northern end it can be portaged for a short distance overland to arrive at saltwater again at Oliver Inlet, a short distance by water from Juneau.

Ed Ramsted, the fellow I agreed to work for on the island, had the previous winter transported his fox pelts by small boat up to the northern end of Seymour Canal. He then carried all the furs overland to another small boat waiting on the Juneau side, which transported him and his furs on into Juneau to be sold there to Goldstein's fur auction house. By making the overland portage he had avoided the much longer trip by water all the distance around Glass Peninsula and through Stephens Passage. Stephens Passage can be extremely rough in winter, and storms can force small boats to delay for days or even weeks.

Fox pelts

Of course, it was necessary for him to make arrangements months in advance to coordinate the arrival and departure of the boats on opposite sides of the portage. The boat on the Juneau side would be picking him up on December twenty-third at Oliver Inlet, and returning him to Oliver Inlet from Juneau on January third. His partner from Dorn Island must travel north to the Seymour Canal side of the portage on January 3rd to meet him as he returned from Juneau. No radio communications were available in those days for small boats so everyone must trust in each others good judgment to be reasonably sure everything worked out well.

It was a mild winter with not much snow, which made it rather a simple job for two men to carry the hundred or more fox pelts overland from saltwater to saltwater in two trips through only knee-deep snow. Ed Ramsted then boarded the Juneau bound boat with the fox pelts while his partner, Cranky Nels, returned to Dorn Island before darkness set in, which is by three p.m. in December.

After selling their furs at auction in Juneau, Ed of course immediately got drunk and stayed that way for nearly a week before sobering up and getting prepared for the return trip back to Oliver Inlet and the portage back over to the Seymour side. He also bought a lot of supplies that were needed at the fox farm and which would have to be carried across the portage in a couple trips. Fortunately very little snow had fallen during his ten days in Juneau, so Ed wore his suit and topcoat plus a new hat he had bought himself as a Christmas gift. His knee-high boots were high enough to avoid most of the snow except for a snowdrift here and there on the trail.

After bidding adieu to his Juneau friend who prepared to return to Juneau before darkness also, he hustled across the portage with his first pack on January third. It was raining half rain and half snow, but his topcoat managed to soak up most of it.

Arriving on the Seymour side he was startled to discover his partner and the boat were nowhere in sight. He dropped his first pack under a big Spruce tree and hurried back over the portage again only to discover that his Juneau transportation was also gone on his return trip to Juneau. There was nothing he could do but load up again with his remaining supplies and tramp back over the portage to the Seymour side, where still no boat was in sight to pick him up for the return to Dorn Island.

The wind and rain were increasing, so all he could do was locate a large spruce tree with protective branches that would shed much of the rain and snow if he must spend the night under it. He had no axe to possibly chop some firewood, but did manage to rip loose some rotten, but half-dry, wood that had lain for years after toppling over from wind. Also, there was pitch oozing down the side of the protective spruce tree that he managed to slice

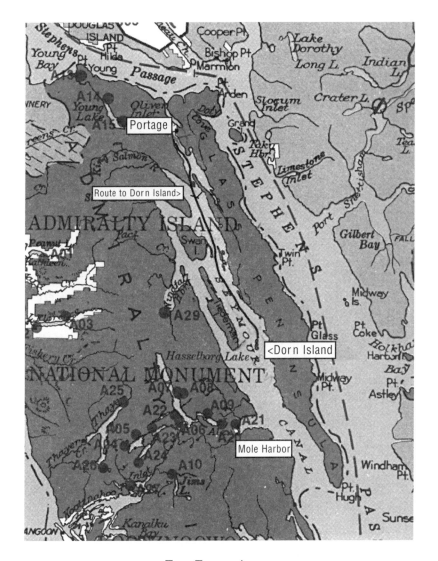

Fox Farm Area

away with his jackknife and make into a small pile on the lee side of the tree. Not being a smoker, he only had a couple matches to expend trying to start a fire.

Darkness was coming on fast now, and in the timber, under his tree, it was darker yet. The only paper he had to start a fire was a couple of receipts for supplies he had bought in Juneau. His first attempt to light a match ended in failure as the wind extinguished the match almost immediately, even before he could ignite his tiny, pitiful two receipts, which possibly were damp also.

Hoping to make his small patch of paper more likely to ignite with his last match, he scoured his pockets again but could only come up with two twenty dollar bills he had in his wallet. Shrugging his shoulders, he placed both of them on his tiny pile of paper and, shielding his last match with his hands, he managed to ignite his forty dollar pile of paper money, which in turn ignited his spruce pitch which managed to create enough heat and warmth to ignite his rotten but half-dry wood and give him a bit of light even if not much heat.

He did have other clothing in his pack which he had worn across the portage December twenty-third carrying the furs. He dug these clothes out now and put on everything he had in layers of clothing to keep warm overnight. Not having enough firewood to allow for a decent larger fire for warmth, he budgeted his remaining woodpile so he could at least keep a small flicker going all night for light. Circling his tree was his only way to keep warm, by going round and round with a short stop now and then to stoke his little fire with a bit of precious firewood to allow him a bit of light. Fortunately, there was no snow at the base of the tree.

The only edible food he had in his pack that did not require cooking was a few pounds of dried prunes and a few pounds of dried apricots. These he took turns munching on as he continued to circle his tree hour after hour, listening to the wind and rain splattering down.

Daylight did not arrive until nearly nine a.m. and his small stockpile of rotten firewood was almost totally depleted, but with daybreak he could manage to whittle more spruce branches with his jackknife to replenish his fire and increase the warmth. At last he had a decent fire going and could allow himself the luxury of leaning up against his protective tree to doze for a few moments until the chill was felt and he must circle some more.

With daylight at last he could also see that the storm was abating and soon perhaps his partner could be putt-putting up to the portage to pick him up in their tiny twenty-five-foot boat with a one cylinder, four horsepower engine. It was about thirty miles from Dorn Island up to the north end of Seymour, which meant at least a five hour trip with fair wind and tide for his partner to get there, or about two p.m. at best. Anyhow, he now had daylight and a decent fire plus adequate prunes and dried apricots to last a couple days if necessary. He had no container to hold water over the fire to make hot tea, though, so must be satisfied with prunes and apricots till help arrived.

About two p.m. he could see a tiny speck, way, way down Seymour Canal, coming in his direction. It gradually got bigger and bigger as it putt-putted along at its best pace. Finally, it arrived with Cranky Nels, his partner, who apologized for not being at the rendezvous a day earlier. The bad weather had not allowed him to risk the rough trip up Seymour. It was again getting dark, so all they could do was load their supplies aboard and commence the long voyage back to Dorn Island. Before they had traversed more than ten miles of their return trip, they had to anchor in the lee of a protective peninsula as darkness came on again. Happy New Year!

Now it was spring again and everything was springing back to life. Cranky Nels had advised Ed that after the winter pelting of their fox furs this next December, he planned to quit the fox farming profession and return to commercial halibut fishing, as the loneliness of being isolated for months on end without any visitors was not for him.

That, of course, was why I was getting the opportunity to learn the ins and outs of fox farming during the spring and summer before Nels left, so I could possibly replace him as Ed's partner. Naturally, there was no mention of wages as the only payday, if any, was after the fox pelts were sold each year about Christmas time. All the year's expenses were deducted from the price the pelts were sold at and, if any money remained, it could then be divided equally between the partners. However, the price of long-haired Blue Fox fur had steadily declined each year as more and more fox pelts were placed on the market for auction due to so many additional individuals entering the fox farming business.

I was very optimistic about it all as I had wished for a long time to be a fox farmer. One would be free of all the demands of living in town with electricity bills, garbage bills, water bills, etc., etc. I thought that being out on an island, away from all the day to day inconveniences in town, would really be a wonderful life.

Departing town in their small little boat with our lifeboat in tow, I felt as if I was at last out and away on a great adventure. Our four horsepower engine putt-putted away at a steady rhythm and, though the fumes from the one cylinder engine were terribly strong due to leaky connections from the exhaust, by sitting back at the stern post to steer at the tiller, one could actually view the scenery as we putt-putted past at our five miles or less per hour. It was about sixty-five miles by water from Petersburg back to Dorn Island, so it was certain we would not arrive in one day. We did finally arrive at Whitney Island in late afternoon, so tied to the mooring and rowed ashore in our small lifeboat to visit.

Whitney Isle was also a fox farm, but the

owners were man and wife who had, through hard work, made it into a comfortable home with most of the conveniences of living in town. We visited with them for a couple hours and were fortunate to be invited for cake and coffee before departing in our rowboat back to our live-aboard boat. The boat had one bunk only, for Ed, so I curled up on the floor under a blanket, with my dog, Kamoke, beside me for warmth.

Starting out early the next morning we had to cross Stephens Passage before entering Seymour Canal. The weather was calm and we had fair tide, so we were able to reach Dorn Island just before dusk. We were visited all along the way by friendly porpoises who zipped around us, almost near enough to touch. Smoke was coming from the house on shore as we anchored our boat, climbed into our skiff, and rowed ashore.

On meeting Ed's partner, Nels, I was surprised that he smiled when shaking my hand in welcome, as he didn't seem "cranky" at all. He had a hot meal of boiled, salted fish ready to eat, as he no doubt had seen us coming for a long time before we arrived. The boiled fish was good, as we hadn't had anything but bread and butter to eat all day, because the fumes inside the boat made it difficult to build a fire in our tiny wood stove. So, on the trip we just ate out in the open air and washed the bread down with water from a barrel on deck. When dusk came, we all three had our own bunks to spread our blankets in, with Kamoke sharing mine. There was no electricity for lights, only a kerosene lamp.

Early the next morning, immediately after breakfast, I was introduced to one end of a long crosscut saw, while Nels took the handle on the other end and we began methodically sawing blocks of wood off a log three feet in diameter.

We sawed while Ed built a big fire under an immense cooker into which he poured water. Then he brought some smoked fish from the smokehouse and cut it up into smaller pieces that were placed in the cooker. Then cereal was scooped from a burlap sack and also added to the mixture in the cooker. Lastly, from a barrel sitting nearby, a deer hide was pulled out of a brine and a potful of deer hair was scraped from the hide and dumped into the cooker. This, Nels explained, was essential for the foxes to eat with their cereal and fish to help prevent them from getting worms.

It all sounded logical to me as I continued pushing and pulling on my end of the crosscut saw. The saw never seemed to move down through the log, if I watched its progress. When I just stared vacantly at the ground or away from the log, eventually another block of wood would finally fall away. It seemed that the wood we were cutting off in blocks, was being split up by Ed and stoked under his cooker faster than we were able to saw the blocks off.

When I inquired as to how often this procedure was repeated, I was a bit disappointed to discover that during the fox pupping time, when the little foxes were being born, the mothers ate ravenously, as did the fathers who seemed to have nothing else to do but sit and bark. They must be fed every other day by rowing around the island in a large, heavy, water-soaked skiff, stopping along the way to carry water and cooked food up to the feed cabins situated about every hundred yards along the way.

On days when it was too windy and rough to row the heavy skiff, we must carry the food in buckets that could be placed on hooks that extended down from a yoke that was placed on the carrier's shoulders, similar to ones used on oxen. I offered to do my share, so Nels carried the heavy buckets of feed, and at each feed shack, I would pour water in the foxes' water basin, then dip feed from the buckets to pour onto their feed pans.

While doing so, I had removed my coat and laid it nearby. I was dismayed to discover a fox had immediately pooped on it. I was reassured by Nels that this was common practice for the foxes as it showed their gratitude for our carrying all this food out to them on our shoulders. I learned as time went by that foxes immediately pooped on anything handled recently by humans, including oar handles, axe handles, clothing, etc.

The weather had been calm and sunny

every day for more than a week now, which meant our water supply was running low. There was no water stream on the island so every bit of rainwater on the roof of the house was diverted by rain trough into a barrel for use, not only by us, but also for cooking feed for the foxes. Toilet facilities were an outhouse that sat near the house. In summer it was reasonably comfortable, but in winter it was strictly functional and one did not tarry there any longer than absolutely necessary.

As the weather remained calm, Ed decided it was a good time to row our heavy skiff across to Glass Peninsula with a load of containers to get fresh water from a small stream flowing down from the mountain. We had two large barrels to be filled using three gallon buckets. We took the buckets up to the stream and dipped bucket after bucket, then carried them back down to our skiff, and emptied them time after time till both barrels were filled. Then we filled the buckets again and the long return trip to Dorn Isle began with two of us rowing in unison, myself at the second seat digging into the water in time, with my oars. The distance was probably less than one mile, but with a heavily loaded, water-soaked skiff it took a good hour or more to cross the water back to the island.

I was beginning to realize how comfortable it had been in town to merely turn a faucet to receive all the water one wished. Now as we returned with our loaded water barrels, it was necessary to reverse the process and pour our water one bucket at a time into the water barrels connected to the rain troughs at the house.

We had been back a week now from town, and, as the following day was Sunday, Ed decided it was time to take our powered boat and putt-putt over to Mole Harbor in hopes some early salmon might be arriving at the salmon stream there. Mr. Allen Hesselborg lived alone there and had done so for twenty years or more. His only company were the local Brown bear that also resided nearby and fed on the salmon that arrived by the thousands from early July until September. Hesselborg would not allow anyone to cross his property with any firearms as he absolutely forbade any bear hunting on his property. His only income was as a big game guide in May and June, then again in September, but never near his own homestead at Mole Harbor, where each bear had been named by him.

His clients were brought out by a large yacht from Juneau that had contracted earlier with hunters from all across America and also Europe. Hesselborg would have the yacht continue on up Seymour Canal to Windfall Harbor to anchor. From there he would use his own outboard boat to take the hunters farther on to wherever he chose to hunt with them. If he decided he disliked any of the hunters, he would immediately return him to the anchored yacht, and refuse to take that particular hunter out again.

Hesselborg's reputation preceded him, and all his hunters were advised to handle him with kid gloves or lose the opportunity of hunting with probably one of the best and most successful guides in Alaska at that time. He was considered an eccentric, which he probably was, as who wouldn't be after living alone with his Brown bear for more than twenty years?

We anchored our own boat down in deep enough water for it to remain afloat, rowed ashore in our small dinghy, and walked for a long, long distance across the Mole Harbor flats until we reached the salmon stream, then walked beside the stream for a bit before his house came into view. Hesselborg was planting potatoes in his garden as if he had been hired by the hour to do so. He barely looked up when we arrived, but acknowledged our presence by nodding to us.

Ed had told me he acted a bit strangely around people, but he certainly knew we were coming to visit long before we arrived at his home, because he scanned the harbor with a twenty power scope whenever any boat entered the bay to be certain no one came ashore with a gun. If anyone was foolish enough to do so, Hesselborg would conceal himself until they passed by, then step out with his own rifle and challenge them to get immediately off his property, which encompassed most of the shoreline of Mole Harbor.

He offered to make us a cup of coffee, but Ed said no as we had only come to see if possibly some early salmon had arrived. Fresh fish was sorely needed to replenish our smoke salmon that was nine months old now and not appetizing to the foxes. Hesselborg said, "No, I haven't seen even the first salmon as of yet," then continued planting his potatoes as if the conversation was ended. We awkwardly began our departure after saying good-bye. A nod was his only response.

We had spent less than an hour at his home, but in that time two huge Brown bear had arrived across the stream, no doubt also looking for salmon. We talked as loudly as we could to each other while also giving as much space to the bear as possible. They merely stood their ground and watched us slink past. We did not run as it might provoke them, but every reflex urged me to do so as we silently put distance between us, without taking even a deep breath. Whatever their names were I was plenty glad to say, "So long," to them. We were plenty relieved to reach our dinghy and retreat to our anchored boat, where we hauled the anchor by hand, and putt-putted back to Dorn Island, where no Brown bear were residing, thankfully!

Ed was eager to somehow get some good fresh bait so we could set our ground-line for fresh fish, not only for ourselves but for the foxes also. He had some salted herring in a barrel, but had no success whatever when using some for his set lines. He had no net to catch the herring that often entered the harbor in the evening and kept flipping till long after dark.

I had raked herring in the harbor of Petersburg for years to sell at fifty cents a bucket to the salmon trollers who utilized them for salmon bait. Noticing a long weathered strip of planking, I asked if Ed cared if I tried to trim it down on one edge so it might swish speedily through the water and be used for raking herring. He agreed and, surprisingly, Cranky Nels dug through his possessions and came out with an Old Country wood plane that he had brought with him from Norway in hopes of perhaps getting a job in the US as a carpenter. He set to planing off the rough, weathered wood on the outside of the strip of plank on each side until he had it trimmed down to about and inch thickness. Then he began planing it wedge shaped on each of the front edges until he had them trimmed down to about a quarter-inch thickness.

We located about two dozen finishing nails which we drove into the quarter-inch leading edge at three-inch intervals for about three feet along the bottom of the strip of wood. It was now a rake. The nails or spikes protruded from the wood about an inch or more depending on the length of our finishing nails and the depth we had hammered them into the wood. The upper handle was rounded off for fitting into a handhold and our rake now looked almost professional. We got busy filing off the nail heads until they were needle sharp and, when finished, we had our own herring rake ready for a school of herring to arrive.

That following evening a small school of herring came into the harbor, and Cranky Nels rowed the heavy, big skiff while I laid out at the bow as far as I could reach without over-balancing, to rake through the herring each time I saw them flashing underwater in a school. We managed to fill up a three gallon bucket before the school became frightened and went deeper to avoid us. I was the Hero of the day as, surprisingly, neither Ed or Cranky Nels had ever considered using a herring rake for getting bait.

The next morning we busily used our herring to bait our halibut hooks that were tied to a line at eighteen-foot intervals to make it convenient for coiling the line. We cut each of the larger herring in two to allow more hooks to be baited. When we used up all our herring, we had to supplement them with enough extra salted herring to finish baiting all the hooks.

We tied a rock on at the start of our line to make it sink to the bottom. Then we rowed out to the southeast end of the island and began rowing offshore. Ed lowered the rock into the water and began back-setting our baited hooks that ran out over an oar he had brought along.

When the final herring had been set over-board attached to our groundline, he attached another rock to that end, about forty pounds of weight, then another float line that allowed him to lower his weighted line to bottom. Once he felt his weighted line reach bottom, he placed a small buoy at the upper end, which floated showing us the beginning of our set gear and where we must begin to pull it back. We had about forty hooks baited so were optimistic we would get fresh fish, hopefully, lots of fresh fish.

We impatiently rowed ashore and walked along the beach to keep warm while waiting a couple of hours for our gear to soak. Then we rowed back to our buoy and commenced pulling it back through an oarlock that was fastened solidly for rowing. The gear did not pull easily, either, until we finally got our rock anchor up to water level and hoisted it aboard by hand.

Then came the first empty hook, then another, and another until many empty hooks had been recoiled into the skiff bottom. At last came a turbot, an ugly little fish, shaped like a small halibut with a grey belly, and a brown back, and razor sharp teeth. It was not very edible but was at least some fresh fish for the foxes. Then a few hooks later came a large skate, also shaped like a halibut, and also not very edible for humans, but the fins could be utilized for fox feed. But, AHA! Ed could feel something large jerking on the line as he pulled, and after several more empty hooks, Lo and Behold, we had a thrashing halibut, weighing about twenty pounds, to gaff aboard and tranquilize by beating him over the head with an oar until he stopped kicking. Another few empty hooks and another smaller halibut became our prize, then another turbot, another few empty hooks, and our first rock anchor was up and taken aboard. We were all happy to have fresh halibut for our dinner, plus enough fresh scrap fish to make a good cooking for the foxes, when we added the head and fins from our halibut.

The next morning it was back to the cross-cut saw as usual, but after our evening meal of fresh halibut, we all seemed jollier. Even Cranky Nels could crack a joke after each wood block rolled clear. The foxes evidently could smell their fresh fish food coming, as we rowed around the shoreline, stopping at each feed house to dole out the mixture. We were careful not to set down any of our clothing for them to pay their respects on either.

The next day Ed suggested that we, too, could plant some potatoes as Mr. Hesselborg was doing. Their own potatoes were mostly sprouting in the sack and had to be peeled at length before they could be boiled. They had tried several times over the years to plant and raise potatoes near the house, but the potatoes had done poorly, perhaps due to poor soil or not enough sunlight, as the trees around the house protected it from the winter Northerly winds, but also kept that part of the island in the shade most of the day. Ed had noticed that a long peninsula, jutting out from the timber near where the fresh water stream entered the bay, had sunlight most of the day. He was sure potatoes might do well there, as grass grew shoulder high there in summer, and skunk cabbage grew there in abundance.

Okay, the next morning we took our spades and axes and our sprouting potatoes, plus a dozen sides of year-old smoked salmon to be utilized as fertilizer, if necessary. The peninsula was sandy soil all right as Ed had predicted, and it made for easy digging after clearing the garden area of new grass and skunk cabbage. By evening all the sprouting potatoes were cut into pieces and planted, making a dozen or more plantings, plus we had chopped up the smoked salmon and buried most of it with the potato sprouts. We had also carried up seaweed from the beach and a few starfish we had captured with an oar to distribute on our potato plants. Feeling satisfied we had done a good day's work, we rowed homeward in our skiff, hungry, but looking forward to another meal of fresh halibut.

The next day it was back to sawing more wood, while Ed did the fox feed cooking. We used up every scrap of our halibut, heads, fins and tails, to supplement the year-old smoked fish we had also cut up and stirred into the cooker with the cereal and deer hair. When it was cooked, we had to again load it all in the heavy old skiff and Cranky Nels and I began rowing to circumnavigate Dorn Island. Our voyage was similar to Magellan's, but he didn't have to stop every so often and feed a damned bunch of hungry foxes that tried their best to leap into the skiff and poop on our oar handles. Damn the rotten bastards!

We returned to the other side of the island only to see Ed motioning to us and pointing across the water towards our potato patch. Dammit, three huge Brown bear were out amongst our plantings digging up all the smoked salmon fertilizer we had so patiently buried to outsmart the crows and ravens. We had no gun to frighten the bear away except for an old .30-.40 caliber Krag rifle, the type used in the Spanish American War by our troops. This rifle had hung on the wall for years without being used and the barrel was completely choked with spider webs from years of spiders camping in it. Ed had depended on his friends coming down to Seymour each fall during deer season and killing enough deer to give him and Cranky Nels all the venison they wanted for eating and salting.

Brown Bear

I took the Krag down off the spikes where it had rested, unfired for so long, and decided to force something through the barrel to dislodge the spider webs. Some old trolling wire someone had thrown away lay out on the beach, and, after a real struggle, I could force this eighth inch wire down the barrel till it could be seen in the gun magazine, where the shell was ejected after firing and replaced with another shell by bolt action.

Removing the trolling wire, I tied a nail to a length of string and dropped that down the barrel till it also came out into the firing chamber. Hauling the string on through till I had enough length to return a piece of cloth back up through the barrel, I made a loop, and Ed cut a piece of wool cloth from one of his old Union suits. Smearing the cloth with lard, I drew it back up the barrel with a host of spider webs clinging to it. Replacing the cloth with another piece of Union suit, I drew it back down the barrel and out the other end, filled again with spider web. Another piece of underwear well smeared with lard was drawn back up the barrel again and so on several more times until the cloth came out reasonably clean. Some oil on the bolt and its mechanism, plus some on the trigger and other parts, and we began to have a .30-.40 Krag just like the one Teddy Roosevelt might have been brandishing as he led the Rough Riders on their charge up San Juan hill in 1898. Who knows?

Now for the ammunition. Ed remembered seeing a couple of shells for the .30-.40 Krag somewhere in one of the drawers, and with some intense looking we finally located two .30-.40 shells that were almost unrecognizable in caliber, because they were so corroded. By patiently sandpapering them lightly, then wiping them off and smearing them with lard, we now had a formidable musket to defend our potato patch. Sure enough, the next afternoon we rowed back across the channel to our potato farm. There were no bear in sight.

Cranky Nels insisted on bringing along some old halibut groundline that we weren't using to make snares to discourage the bear if they returned, as he had seen done in Norway as a young man. The bear had really wreaked havoc on our potato planting as they had already dug up about half our planting while digging for the smoked salmon. Ed had sensibly brought along additional potato sprouts, so we again sliced them apart and replanted most of the excavations the bear had made in our patch. In the meantime, Nels was setting up his snares between the trees that bordered our potato patch along the route he assumed the bear would need to take if they ever returned again.

We returned to the island, but not to anymore fresh halibut for dinner as it was all gone. We had to settle for soaked-out salted venison, which, I for one, was getting plenty sick and tired of eating. I was all for shooting a deer if one showed up on the beach across by our potatoes, but Ed cautioned me that our prized .30-.40 Krag might just explode backward instead of forward because of its condition. I wondered if Teddy Roosevelt had to ponder this also as he charged up the hill.

Now if some herring would again come flipping back into the harbor, we might possibly rake enough again to bait our gear. None had shown up for several days, as they possibly might have warned all other herring to beware. "Some idiot up at Dorn Island has a long pole with spikes on the bottom end he keeps sweeping through the water anytime a herring shows its face."

The next day it was back to my position at the end of a two-man crosscut saw again. It seemed to be a never-ending job, trying to keep ahead of the house stove and the huge cooker for fox feed. Then back to the skiff to row and row around the island with more feed for the foxes. When we had circled the island again, and were back on the east side where we could look across at our potato patch, there were the three big bear again, looking about the size of buffalo. I doubt any Indian would gallop up beside one of these bear though, to shoot an arrow into him. Mr. Bear would quite likely grab the Indian's horse by one leg and proceed to tear the horse apart for dinner while the Indian and his bow and arrow beat a hasty retreat.

Ed was at home also looking across at our potato patch with disgust. I insisted that we take the Krag rifle and row back over before evening to see if we couldn't frighten the bear away before they excavated the whole potato planting. Ed was reluctant, as he believed in "live and let live," which is an excellent philosophy as long as all participants live up to it, but these damned bear were over there tear-ing up our efforts at farming, and must be frightened away somehow.

We all three piled back into the heavy, old skiff and Nels and I each took our seats and began rowing in unison as hard as we could. We depended on Ed, who was sitting down staring ahead, to give us directions to keep us heading in the correct route to our potato planting. When he began shaking his head nervously, I pulled in my oars to avoid tangling them with Nels', who continued rowing as hard as he could without turning around to view our garden. There stood three huge bear, all three sporting halibut gear neckties. Evidently Nels' snares had merely given them more incentive to dig up the remainder of our garden.

I yelled at Nels to stop rowing, as we were almost near enough to bump the shore with three angry bear standing their ground with no apparent thought of running away either. We all began yelling at them, but that only made them come closer for a better look at us. I was all for firing a shot in the air with our Krag rifle, but Ed nixed that idea, fearing it might only antagonize them further. The distance was perhaps one hundred and fifty feet, and, obviously, these three bear had never been shot at or even frightened by man. After all, they had been the Kings of Admiralty Island for thousands of years before the White Man arrived.

The Indians had lived peaceably with the

bear for generations by each leaving the other alone. Now came the upstart White Man who decided that he was to be the new King of Admiralty. Obviously these three bear hadn't heard about the White Man king yet and still considered themselves boss of Admiralty.

All of us in that heavy skiff came to the same conclusion at once, and, without saying one word, rowed backwards quietly so we could keep the bear in view until we were well out in deep water again, and they didn't look quite so formidable to us. Then, silently, without speaking another word, we rowed back to Dorn Island in defeat. We did not return again to view our potato planting until no bear had appeared in it for several days. With one hasty look, we were convinced all our plantings had been dug up and strewn all over the area, and it was hopeless to attempt any more farming except on Dorn Island where, hopefully, no bear would swim half a mile or more to eat our fish fertilizer.

This retreat from our planting had a sobering effect on us all, but there was more to come. Ed regularly walked all over Dorn Island to see how the little fox pups were doing. When he came back, he was usually carrying one, or sometimes two, little dead pups that had either crawled out of the den and died, or, more likely, the mother fox had herself dragged the dead pup away from the other pups so they might have more space. Undoubtedly the Bald eagles had also retrieved any dead pups they sighted for food for their young eaglets. How many more they also swooped down and flew away with that were not dead was a good question.

Ed had sighted very, very few live pups when we carried food up to the feed stations. The pups should have begun coming out of the dens to feed beside their parents by now. We had managed again to rake enough herring to bait our groundline and again catch welcome fresh halibut and other scrap fish to make the fox food more desirable. However, much of the food was being left uneaten, which meant to Ed that there weren't near the mouths to feed that he had anticipated. He began to become more and more discouraged with discovering so many dead fox pups with no apparent reason for their deaths.

Years later it was discovered that every island fox farm sooner or later became infected with lung worms, whether from a diseased fox or perhaps from the damp dens the foxes were forced to inhabit on a small island with no other choice of a better den site.

However, it was obvious that our fox pelting the following December would not even manage to pay the annual expenses just for food and upkeep on the island. It had now been more than a month since we had left Petersburg, and the glamour of fox farming was rapidly evaporating for me. Returning to town to look for some type of work looked more and more attractive each day. I had promised Ed I would stay on even though the work was hard, but now working from daybreak to dark, with no hope of earning even a small wage, was very discouraging.

I began considering patching up an old abandoned skiff that had sat for some time with water running in and out of it every time the tide rose and fell. I even kept telling myself I was repairing the old skiff so we could have another spare skiff if needed. I had no caulking, but found some more old halibut groundline and unbraided some of it to use for caulking up the wide seams that had lost their rotted caulking over the years.

I managed to finally get the skiff floating well enough that it was useable, but it needed bailing constantly to remain afloat. I then spoke with Ed about the possibility of my rowing this old skiff back to Petersburg, which might take a week or more. My dog even seemed to perk up at the thought of departing Dorn Island. I kept climbing each day to the highest part of the island to look for a passing boat, as did Robinson Crusoe, who was also stranded on an island. I hoped to sight a fishing boat that might possibly be returning to Petersburg.

Ed noticed that I was by now really getting desperate to return to town and find some kind of a paying job. He nixed the idea of my rowing the old, rotten, heavy skiff as there were open stretches of water to be crossed, some of them several miles across that could get very rough in sudden squalls, even for a powered boat. He advised me that he would get a list ready of supplies they would soon be needing and take my dog and me back to town.

In a few more days, he said we would be departing the next morning, early, to putt-putt across Stephens Passage again on our homeward journey. I had been connected almost daily to one end of their crosscut saw and had decided that somehow, no matter what, I would earn enough money so that I need never, ever again saw a damned block of wood for heat or cooking.

As the time came to depart, I shook hands with Nels, who had really never once been at all cranky with me. I could see that somehow he really hated to see me and my dog leaving, as the two of us had made their lonely existence a bit more exciting at times. I would miss them also, but I was young and anxious to make money so I, too, could buy a boat with an engine and, hopefully, become a successful fisherman.

Our trip back to Petersburg was rather uneventful as the weather remained calm all the way, which I realized would have been very fortunate for me, if I had started out rowing a heavy, water-soaked skiff the sixty-five miles back to town across all this open water. When Petersburg finally came into view on the third day, I never had realized how wonderful the docks and floats and boats looked as we putt-putted into the harbor. What a welcome sight it was. Sixty years later, I can look back with fondness at some of the experiences I had on the six weeks at Dorn Island, but sawing wood with a crosscut saw was not one of them.

After my venture into fox farming it became obvious there was no quick or easy way to make my fortune. I took no interest in prospecting for gold because I had observed prospectors all my life, coming and going from their secret diggings looking for another legendary Lost Rocker. None that I knew had ever located enough gold to even pay Sing Lee, a local store owner, for grubstaking them.

Long-lining for halibut in season seemed the only available possibility for one anxious to somehow get going at making a living. I had seventy-five dollars saved from the sale of the *Hobo* a year before, to use for a down payment on a better boat I had seen for sale in the harbor.

Part 3

Working the Saltwater

9

*"He always wore his riding breeches and
leather leggings, plus a ten gallon hat.
His leather or seal skin vest was open so
his gold watch chain with a huge gold
nugget was always visible, and he had
assorted ivory handled jackknives dangling from his belt."*

The Shrimp King

Earl Ohmer arrived in Petersburg in 1916
with his shrimp boat, *Kiseno*. He had
made a prospecting tour through parts of the
British Columbia coastline looking for a likely
site to establish a shrimp processing plant. His
goal was to locate his plant near enough to a
year round supply of shrimp, that each day's
catch could be returned to his processing plant
that day for hand picking. Prince Rupert, B.C.,
initially looked promising with plenty of available
labor. However, after a short period of experi-
mental shrimp trawling in the area, he decided
to move farther north looking for more protected trawling areas where fishing would not
be disrupted by foul weather during winter
storms. The Petersburg area appeared to be a
promising place to settle, with protected bays
and inlets nearby, and good quantities of available
shrimp.

It was necessary to construct the processing plant far out on the tide flats where the
water was deep enough to allow his trawlers

to unload their catch at any stage of tide, plus deep enough to accommodate larger freight boats that arrived periodically to load his hand-picked, canned shrimp for shipment south to Seattle. His plant adjoined the Citizens' Public Dock where the Pacific Steamship Company leased space for unloading additional freight for other local businesses in town.

With no cold storage facilities available in Petersburg until 1927, it was necessary to dry pack his shrimp product in sealed cans to preserve it until it arrived in Seattle where it could then be transported by railway to all parts of the continental United States.

With adequate supplies of shrimp to be trawled nearby and a steady supply of shrimp pickers available, Ohmer's plant flourished, and his fleet of trawlers increased in numbers over the years to nearly a dozen. Under his trade name of Alaska Glacier Seafood, Ohmer also dabbled somewhat in purchasing halibut that he iced in wood boxes with glacier ice chopped from easily available icebergs that drifted ashore from the nearby Le Conte Glacier.

His work force steadily increased to accommodate the large amount of shrimp now being unloaded daily for hand picking. More picking tables and benches were acquired for the shrimp pickers who sat side by side shelling the cocktail shrimp. Pickers were paid by the picked weight they completed each day.

In the winter months, when no other pro-

Earl Ohmer and Trophy

cessor operated for salmon, Ohmer's cannery
had shrimp pickers pleading for employment,
even though most could only pick enough poundage
at ten cents per picked pound, to make a bare
existence. In summer during the salmon canning season, his pickers evaporated to work in
the salmon canneries for better paying jobs.

The exceptions were some of the fastest hand pickers, mostly of Asian descent, who stayed on year round and became Ohmer's steady dependable crew as years went by.

It was necessary to govern the number of daily pickers who showed up each day to work. This was done by posting, each evening, on a blackboard hung on the town side of the long dock, the total amount of shrimp caught, and unloaded, by trawlers for the following day's processing. This allowed the pickers the options of coming to the plant when enough shrimp were available to allow for a full day's work for a full crew, or only enough available for half a crew of pickers. The pickers themselves made the decision.

Drinking water was available only at a faucet out at the entrance to the shrimp cannery with a cup placed nearby for the convenience of thirsty workers. No washing facilities were available at all outside, but a faucet was available inside the picking room for anyone choosing to rinse their hands off before going home or when returning to their picking position from the toilet.

Two, large, three-seater, outside toilets were placed outside the shrimp picking room, one for men and one for women. Outdated Sears & Roebuck and Montgomery Ward catalogs were available inside for perusing, if one chose, while occupying one of the three-hole seating arrangements. Privacy at the toilets was rather limited as both toilets had been constructed originally of newly sawed lumber that had shrunk, of course, over the seasons allowing for an inch or more of space between the boards. This provided ventilation, but also allowed one to check through the large cracks before going in to see if seating space was available. When the tide was low and the water had receded, looking down one of the three holers to the tide line below created a dizzying effect.

Many of the shrimp cannery's Indian shrimp pickers lived in floathouses near the cannery. These floathouses were constructed on large logs that made them float when the tide was up. All the floathouses had their own outhouse or toilet set out, usually at the very extreme end of their log float. Most merely had a wall constructed about six feet high to shield the occupant from view of his neighbors nearby. However, when the tide was completely out, these same outhouses sat high and dry on the mud flats. Because these outhouses had no roof, a person on the dock could sometimes look down directly into the outhouse whether occupied or not.

On weekends, many of us kids would wander down the long, long dock that stretched out across the mud flats that were nearly completely bare when the tide was out. When we kids were strolling past on the dock, if snow was available on the dock, we'd get an irresistible urge to make up snowballs and test our trajectory at lobbing a few snowballs into an occupied outhouse. The startled occupant would yell in dismay.

The unfortunate occupant was pinned down in the outhouse by us kids, unseen and unrecognized high above them. It was probably difficult for them to decide whether to leap up and run for shelter with their pants down, or cower against the wall and hope for an eventual cease fire.

The head of one household was a mean-looking individual with a big handlebar mustache. Often after being besieged in his own outhouse by our accuracy, he would yank up his pants and come roaring out, amidst a hail of snowballs, running to try and cut us off on the dock before we could escape. Fortunately for us, he had to clamber up the ramp to reach the dock which allowed us to get up momentum and scatter out on main street. He would stand on the street corner, glaring from behind his mustache, while we innocents strolled along window-shopping at the various stores, prepared to dive inside any available store if he recognized any of us and made an effort to catch us and kick our butts.

Earl Ohmer employed many workers year round or seasonally. Fred Porter was one of these. He had been the first skipper of the first shrimp trawler Earl Ohmer owned, the *Kiseno,* and brought the boat up from Washington, prospecting along the way for likely sites for a shrimp plant. Fred had lost an arm several years earlier in an accident at a Washington sawmill, but had been outfitted with a retractable hook for the missing arm. He could do nearly as well with his hook as others could do with a regular arm.

Unfortunately, while hauling back the shrimp trawl he accidentally caught the sleeve of his good arm in the shrimp winch, and before his crewman could rush up and stop the winch, he had destroyed that arm nearly to his shoulder. Fortunately, the crewman had enough experience to place a tourniquet on his damaged arm and proceed back to Petersburg, nearly three hours away. No radio communications were available in those days and the only medication on the boat that could calm Fred somewhat on the long trip was one hand-rolled cigarette after another. The crewman continually rolled the cigarettes while Fred sat on a bench in the pilothouse, leaning against the wall to avoid collapsing, and lighting each new cigarette off the used one. Survive he did, but the arm was so badly mangled it was unusable ever again.

Unable to captain a shrimp trawler, Fred was placed in charge of day to day operations at the shrimp cannery, where he remained until his retirement many years later. He did the weighing of each worker's daily output of picked shrimp, by first setting their containers on the scales, then adjusting the scales for accuracy with his hook.

Bill Stafford was another worker that Earl Ohmer kept around the shrimp plant for many years. Bill worked as an all around handy man doing small construction jobs such as making additional picking tables and benches for seating additional pickers, and keeping the outside toilets in repair. When Bill Stafford was not needed for work at the shrimp plant, he was often sent out to various bays noted for excellent clam digging to buy clams from the clam diggers there.

Although Bill Stafford could neither read nor write, he would make identifying marks for each clam digger's output when weighed and purchased, by carving a notch or a cross in a piece of wood that was then attached to their clam sacks. Only he could identify each person's sacks of clams, but in many years of operations for Ohmer, I never heard of any serious mistakes by Bill Stafford and his method of bookkeeping.

He was very sensitive about being unable to read or write though, and would use any pretense to keep from having it known. "What's the name of that boat going past, Johnny?" he would often ask me when I happened to be down on the shrimp dock on weekends. "My eyes are getting so bad I just can't make her out." When I told him the boat's name, he would always answer, "Oh yes, of course, now I can read it clear too."

Earl Ohmer financed others who wished to go prospecting for gold during summer months, then return to work at the shrimp plant again when the weather turned foul. He was a major investor in the Maid of Mexico gold mine that worked continuously with a small crew for many, many years until World War II began. He was also major owner of the Yukon Fur Farm which was located directly across Wrangell Narrows from his shrimp plant. This location allowed the plant to utilize most of the scrap fish caught by the shrimp trawlers that would otherwise have been unusable. Anyone with a Hard Luck story could always be certain of a five dollar bill from Earl to tide them along in hard times.

No doubt many of the employees at Ohmer's shrimp plant were not necessary to keep operations going, but Earl Ohmer was one who would never turn anyone away, even if it was taking money out of his own pocket to keep them on the work force. Without question, he should have been a very wealthy man for his shrimp plant was doing exceptionally well, but he remained always an employer who survived from one week until the next on the brink of bankruptcy.

His mode of dressing was absolutely distinctive in Southeastern Alaska. He always wore his riding breeches and leather leggings, plus a ten gallon hat. His leather or seal skin vest was open so his gold watch chain with a huge gold nugget was always visible, and he had assorted ivory handled jackknives dangling from his belt.

Over the years his office became more and more cramped with stuffed animals that were sent to him as gifts by taxidermist friends. He had a goose on top of his desk, an owl sitting nearby, and other assorted animals crammed into any available nook and cranny. There was barely space for his secretary to squeeze into her chair amidst all the artifacts that had been loaded onto her desk for lack of any more space on Earl's. How she ever managed to keep her accounts accurately is a mystery, for the office was always crammed with visitors talking with Earl, amidst a blue cloud of tobacco smoke from his pipe.

I never heard a harsh word said about Earl Ohmer, for he was everyone's friend, on a first name basis. His friends included not only local people and those he knew through his business interests, but many others he met while serving over the years on the Petersburg City Council and as chairman of the Alaska Game Commission.

10

"No one really dared spend too much time away from their boat as that young idiot with the Hobo might decide to make his daily trial run and then return for a crash landing while attempting to moor beside them."

Maiden Voyage of the Refloated Hobo

Jobs were nonexistent in Petersburg in 1933. The Depression was being felt even in Alaska which had mostly missed the deep hardship felt in the forty-eight states since the market collapse in 1929. Fish prices had tumbled to their lowest in years, but a fisherman could receive credit at the local markets for staples if he continued fishing during the open seasons and managed to pay his food bills at the close of the fishing season.

With no chance, it appeared, for any kind of a job on shore, I was determined to get into the fishing business to earn money for my last two years of high school in Petersburg. Fishing in an open skiff by rowing I had managed to catch some halibut with groundline gear I had been given by a larger commercial halibut boat that had discarded it as too worn and chaffed for further use on a power gurdie. Trolling for king salmon with the same skiff and oar power, I had managed by midsummer to earn forty dollars. It was obvious that to do better it was necessary to either rent a boat with power, which I couldn't afford, or try to locate some hulk of a boat with an engine that had been beached by the previous owner as too worn-out for further investment.

Just such an outfit lay on its side with the tide running in and out of it twice daily up on Hammer's Slough in the midst of Petersburg. Knowing very little about boats, and less about one with an engine, particularly one that was underwater half of the time, I needed advice from someone with some knowledge before proceeding any further with discussion of a price for same with the owner.

I knew an old gentleman named Wash Bain who I was sure could give me his opinion of the worth of this hulk of a boat, or tell me to forget about it if it was beyond repair. After some difficulty I managed to locate Wash. He was living in a small cabin located out behind some other buildings. It had once been used as a storage shack for odds and ends. Wash had somehow made it livable for himself. He survived by digging clams for crab bait for commercial crabbers, a backbreaking job that paid very little for an educated person like Wash. He had migrated to Alaska from Rhode Island where he had formerly had a family. He never divulged the reason he had left his family to come north to work at menial jobs.

I was pleased to have him say he would of course be glad to come down and survey this boat when the tide was out and it was possible

The Refloated Hobo

to climb up on its deck to look inside. What we saw were two greasy masses of rust, one the engine, the other the stove, which had both been submerged half the time since the boat had been laid to rest a couple months earlier.

After Wash had looked at the hull outside, and also the bottom where salt water was still trickling out the seams from the earlier high tide, he advised me to see if I could turn the flywheel over. I attempted to turn the flywheel by hand, as self-starters were yet unheard of except for automobiles, but was unable to twist it over by hand power. Wash got back on solid ground beside the hull and advised me to not consider paying a dime for this hulk until I had determined if the engine could be salvaged. He told me how to do this. As for the hull itself, he thought there was a possibility it could be recaulked and the boat once again refloated to begin another career.

I was of course anxious to see if the engine could be salvaged so hurried to follow his instructions before the tide came in again. First I went to the oil dock and bought a gallon of cylinder oil and returned to the hull with oil and a wrench that I had borrowed. I then unscrewed the spark plug and peered down into the cylinder. It appeared dry on top of the piston. I poured a cupful of cylinder oil in anyway, then used the wrench again to unscrew one of the engine bolts at the engine base. This allowed at least a quart of liquid to drain out, some oil, some water. Seizing the flywheel again I twisted with all my strength and was elated to finally get the flywheel to revolve slightly, then a bit more. I twisted back and forth and each time I gained a bit more area on the flywheel until at last it could be turned completely around and around. The oil had obviously lubricated the dry cylinder wall.

Now I knew that at last I might become the owner and captain of my own boat, if I was fortunate enough to make a deal for the right price with the owner. By now, however, the tide was again returning and unless I could commence bailing immediately, my hopes for making a transaction for said boat that day were fading as the water rose up to the engine again. I had only time to replace the engine bolt and the spark plug before I had to abandon the sinking ship for I was without a bucket for bailing.

I hurried over to Wash Bain's shack to tell him the good news about the engine, and he nodded and suggested that perhaps, if the price was right, I might make a deal with the owner. He asked me how much money I could afford to invest in buying this boat, and I sadly told him I had a bit less than forty dollars to my name. He advised me to wait till the tide was completely high before making an offer of twenty-five dollars to the owner who would probably again view his boat before considering to sell or refuse my offer.

That is exactly what the owner did, but only the very tip of the cabin was showing above water, making for a discouraging view of the property he was selling. After some thought, he advised me he thought the boat even in its submerged condition, was well worth fifty dollars. I gulped and would have offered my forty dollars lifetime savings except Wash Bain had cautioned me to not offer a dime over twenty-five dollars and insist it was all I had. This I did, but the owner said he would need time to consider my offer and would advise me later.

I waited the next couple days almost sick with desperation watching my hopes and dreams getting submerged every tide, but unable to do anything about it as Wash Bain had cautioned me not to lift a finger towards caulking or attempting to improve anything whatsoever on the boat until my offer was either accepted or refused. He also instructed me to appear rather disinterested in whether the owner did either. This was a lie, as my stomach was in a complete turmoil for fear that he was surely going to refuse my offer.

The second day of agonized waiting for his answer, I saw the owner walk up to again view his partially submerged boat. I managed to arrive there shortly after, accidentally, of course, as to not make him think I was waiting for his answer. No doubt he could tell that I was anxious to find out whether I was about to become a boat owner or was to remain one of the unfortunates who wander the shores forever with dashed hopes.

He again asked if I could only produce twenty-five dollars cash, as the propeller alone was worth that much. I assured him that was all I had, with no hopes for anymore unless I could locate a boat with an engine that operated. Looking once more at his possession, that was rapidly disappearing every moment as the tide rose higher, he nodded and said, "Okay, you just became the proud owner of the vessel *Hobo*."

I was almost overcome with relief, and handed over my twenty-five dollars immediately before he could change his mind. He scribbled a bill of sale on a sheet of paper, shook my hand, and walked away. I just sat down on the shoreline completely entranced with my dreams of the future with the *Hobo* under my command, once the tide went out again, of course.

Now I could hurry back to tell Wash Bain of my good fortune. He advised me to get help from some of my friends who could help with bailing the *Hobo* to keep it afloat, while I towed it to Sing Lee's gridiron behind my skiff. I would need to row with all my strength to make headway. On the gridiron it could be tied snugly to the piling to settle back down again as the tide receded. This would leave it sitting in an upright position for caulking.

I enlisted my two good friends Mike and Bill to help me bail and row the *Hobo* out of Hammer's Slough, the graveyard of several boats, and over to the gridiron. The gridiron was placed directly behind Sing Lee's store where one could buy caulking, nails, tar, and even paint, if one owned a yacht.

It was necessary to commence bailing sea-water from the *Hobo* as the tide rose. Bill, Mike, and I were all kept occupied bailing continuously to hold back the water entering the hull through all the leaking seams. However, as we held our own with the increasing tide the *Hobo* became buoyant and then even began slowly to right itself until, BEHOLD, it was apparent it could again float right side up!

Once the *Hobo* became upright it soon floated

free of the bottom and I hurried to retrieve its anchor. The anchor had been placed up ahead of the boat behind a large rock making it difficult to haul aboard, but it had been included in the sale of the boat and was a necessity for anchoring offshore. Other lines that had held the *Hobo* captive to shore were cast off, and we were on our way out to sea, or at least on our way.

With me rowing steadily towing the *Hobo,* it soon became obvious that the two bailers were unable to hold their own with the incoming leaks, and were now bailing desperately to even keep afloat. This spurred me on to greater efforts, and I began digging as deep as possible with my oars to get more power from each stroke. Every few minutes, I would leap up from rowing sitting down, whirl around and keep rowing standing up just to make certain we were heading in the right direction. This would give me a bit of a break momentarily as I changed from pulling on the oars to pushing on the oars.

Billy and Mike enjoyed no such luxury. They were now bailing for their very lives just to stay afloat and yelling constantly at me "For Christ's sake, hurry up," as they were sinking steadily.

Inching slowly ahead, it became questionable whether Sing Lee's gridiron was an obtainable goal on one tide, or if it was necessary to beach my recent investment and let the tide recede and gravity remove the surplus water.

It was calm, fortunately, and though the *Hobo* was drawing more and more water, we also were moving slowly nearer and nearer towards our goal.

At the halfway mark I shouted back encouragement to my two helpers, who had no time to look up at the scenery even for a moment as they bailed for their lives. I too, was stirring the water with my oars as rapidly as possible to keep making headway for the grid. At last our goal came into view as we rounded the piling and slipped under Ohmer's dock taking a necessary shortcut to remain afloat. I was afraid my two bailers might have leaped ashore, if I had been stupid enough to take the long way around the dock and passed by with the floats so temptingly near.

Anyway, at last we reached safety and were able to wrap our lines around the piling of Sing Lee's gridiron, and though the water continued to pour into the *Hobo*, now there were three bailing buckets in action as my towing had ceased with our arrival. The three of us managed to keep even with the incoming water which we continued bailing until the Hobo's keel had touched down on solid gridiron timbers making it impossible for the *Hobo* to sink any lower. Then as the tide dropped the water inside the hull began retreating with the tide. What a relief! Once we were firmly aground, I rowed my two helpers ashore, thanking them for their help and assuring them they were to be along with me on the maiden voyage of the

Hobo as my guests. They were too exhausted to answer, but grunted, which I considered to be in excited anticipation of the event.

As the tide dropped, I made arrangements with Wash Bain to come down after the water had receded from under the grid and the beach was bared, so we could work at caulking the seams. He gave me a list of the items necessary for this task. Most were available a Sing Lee's store, cotton caulking, oakum, tar, paraffin, and even shingles, as it was possible there were some larger seams too immense for mere caulking. We did not have caulking irons, but Wash promised to bring along his hatchet and a handful of kindling in case a fire was needed to melt the paraffin. The paraffin would be mixed with a portion of tar and smeared over the caulked seams to ensure a watertight finish to our caulking.

Wash arrived just as he had promised, as soon as the water had left the beach bare, and began immediately driving cotton and oakum into every seam as all needed repair. Soon it was necessary for me to run to the store for more oakum and cotton as the repair job was much larger than Wash had anticipated. I was kept busy with the handsaw cutting off the protrusions of shingle wherever they occurred. It took the total thickness of one shingle plus an additional partial shingle sometimes to fill up the seam. Once Wash had completed one side of the *Hobo,* we moved his site of operations to the other side, keeping all his equipment up on the grids out of the mud.

Wash had me get a small bonfire started and place a two-pound coffee can partially filled with tar as close as possible to the fire for heating without being so close it might ignite and burn. He set me to paring strips of paraffin similar to potato peelings into this half-filled can of tar. The paraffin began to melt into the tar once the can became heated. I continually stirred this concoction, being careful it didn't ignite, until Wash called for it. He smeared this mixed sealant over his finished seams with an old paintbrush he had located somewhere.

Now the tide was returning, again making it difficult and soon impossible to keep the bonfire lit. Fortunately, Wash wore boots so was able to keep dry. I wasn't so fortunate, but was so eager to see the job completed I would have swam if necessary to get it done. Once the tide had covered the ground to knee depth, Wash completed his work of caulking the largest seams needing attention. He probably might have continued to finish all the seams, but his boots leaked above knee depth. I was also beginning to shiver from being soaked from no boots whatever. He took another look at the work we had finished and pronounced the *Hobo* "seaworthy!"

I gratefully thanked him and gave him five of my remaining fourteen dollars for his excellent work. He left to return home while I remained to watch as the tide rose to see if our work had really made the *Hobo* more or less watertight. As the tide steadily rose I was elated to see only a small trickle here and there entering the inside of the hull needing only a few buckets now and then of bailing. Wash had assured me that as time progressed our shingles and other caulking would expand making our leaky seams more watertight.

Once the *Hobo* was afloat, I saw no need to remain on the gridiron, as it was apparent I could keep it afloat by bailing it dry every three or four hours until the leaks stopped over time. I connected it again to a towline and once again began rowing, towing my ship to the city float.

I arrived in the skiff slightly ahead of the *Hobo* which was coming behind on a towline. It arrived shortly though and, of course, crashed into the nearest unfortunate who had made the mistake of mooring in the path of my latest acquisition. He came roaring topside in his underwear, as by now it was pitch dark and near midnight. I decided I did not prefer to tie my boat up to a crank like that anyway, so pulled it along farther to tie up beside a fine old friend, who welcomed me even at midnight soaking wet with my boat trailing behind me. I'm sure he had some worries about my prized possession sinking again while it was tied to his boat and causing him problems, but he never mentioned such a thing.

My next project was to somehow try and remove some of the grease and marine growth that had accumulated over the past several months when my boat had been submerged. I used bucket after bucket of cold, soapy water as I had no workable stove. The stove needed stove pipe inside and out before being usable. The woodwork began to slowly appear from under all the grease and oil, and looked as if sometime in the past a coat of paint had once been applied. After many, many trips to a water outlet to get fresh water for scrubbing, I was finally able to stand up without my feet going out from under me from all the grease and slime.

Now I needed advice concerning the one-cylinder engine and how to make it operational. For this I went to Sore Nose Thompson's machine shop. He had acquired his nickname, I presume, because due to some malignancy most of his nose was gone except for one partial section with both nostril holes left bare to the world. He advised me to tow it over to a small float beside his machine shop where he could look himself and decide what might be needed to once again revive the motor. Because his float went dry at low water, I was kept busy each day towing the *Hobo* back and forth from the city float in hopes that one day soon he might consider coming down and giving his professional advice. Finally he had free time, and came aboard to look.

His first efforts were to get down with a wrench and unbolt the big brass carburetor from the engine. He took the carburetor out on deck and poured rusty salt water out of it while advising me it was necessary to take the carburetor up to his shop for cleaning. I, in the meantime, could occupy myself by draining the gas tank which undoubtedly was also full of salt water.

This I did, and he was correct, the gas tank was filled to capacity with salt water. Fortunately, it was placed at the side of the boat and higher than the engine, so that it could feed gasoline to the engine by gravity rather than need a pump to do so.

There apparently had never been a vent pipe to allow air to the fuel tank. This was of course necessary, but being desperately short of money, I elected to circumvent this additional piping by stuffing a potato in the vent opening. This apparently allowed enough air to pass by to give a steady flow of gasoline to the engine.

A coil and a battery were needed for ignition. I bought a battery on credit at the marine supply store where I had credit. Sore Nose Thompson provided a coil at half price. It had been used by someone else in years gone by. It was a Ford coil such as was used in Model T Fords, and when connected to a battery and then to a timer would allow a tremendous jolt of electricity to flow from it to the spark plug. One had to beware of ever foolishly touching the outside of this coil when it was thus connected, as it had a kick like a mule.

I installed my new Hot Shot Dry battery in

a small box nailed to the ceiling as Thompson advised, where it remained safe and dry even if the *Hobo* filled with water through misfortune. Thompson also advised me to pour five gallons of fresh gasoline into the clean fuel tank, leaving a quart of gasoline remaining in the can for priming the engine before starting. This could be done by pouring gasoline from a priming can down through the priming cup, a brass receptacle with a small turnable bar on the side that could be opened and closed to allow gasoline to run through and down onto the top of the piston. I poured cylinder oil into an oil cup on the front of the engine where it could be timed to drip one drop of oil regularly into the cylinder wall of the engine when it was operating, or snapped off when the engine was not in operation. With all this preliminary work completed, all that was remaining was for Thompson to have free time to return with my carburetor when he wished to do so.

Finally the day arrived, and he told me to have the *Hobo* over at his float at high water so he could install the carburetor and coil and connect same to their respective fittings. This done, he poured a small portion of the remaining gasoline from the gas can into another empty one pound coffee can, and squeezed the top of the can into a spout shape. He then poured the gasoline down into the priming cup, from which it drained into the engine.

He nodded through his pipe smoke for me to commence twisting on the flywheel which was twenty-four inches in diameter and directly at the front of the engine. This I did over and over, but nothing happened. Again Thompson opened the priming cup but this time he first poured a tablespoon of cylinder oil into the coffee can of gas and revolved the can until the oil and gas mixed completely. He poured this mixture down the priming cup again and nodded to me to commence twisting the flywheel over. With the first twist I was certain I felt life commence under my hands, but it took another twist before it was definite. There truly is life after death.

My engine sprang to life and the flywheel continued turning faster without my help. What a miracle to really see something once again running that had been left to submerge for months. Thompson retarded the engine somewhat, and then he retreated outside into the fresh air leaving me behind to just stare and marvel at what I owned. Thompson then put his head inside and indicated that the engine was also getting coolant water. The water was pumped through the engine and then returned into the exhaust to be forced overboard through the side of the boat where it appeared as steam. Gad! What a marvel of ingenuity, and to think I owned it all.

I was overcome by it all until I heard Thompson shouting for me to shut the engine off. The heat from the operating engine was making all the old grease in it start melting and smoking until it was almost choking him to be near it. I did as he told me, removing one of the wires from the battery and getting a kick at the same time from the coil. There was no switch to cut off the power to the engine, and probably every boat owner at that time did likewise to stop their engine.

I struggled out on deck into clean fresh air with my ears ringing from the racket the engine made when it was operating. Thompson advised me to allow the engine to cool a bit before again restarting it, and allow time for the smoke to escape out the door. I had at no time been out on deck when the engine was running, but Thompson assured me that we had been tugging at our tie lines which meant, of course, that the shaft to the propeller was connected. This meant that the *Hobo* was liberated once it was untied with the engine operating.

It had no clutch, so it was necessary to get untied and positioned in the correct direction before twisting the flywheel and getting the engine started. This called for some swift timing when my dog, Kamoke, and I were alone. Once the engine started, it was necessary for me to make a running dive back into a small opening at the stern, called a cockpit, where the rudder was attached.

There was a steering wheel, but it was not connected. It could be connected later, if and when I earned enough money to buy chain for this added comfort. For the present all I could do was take my chances of steering back at the stern until I felt I was getting dangerously close to impact with a moored boat, at which time, I would leap from the cockpit and run forward to tear the wire loose from the battery to stop the engine and let the *Hobo* continue on under its own momentum. I hoped to lasso the float or grab the sides of someone's moored boat as I swept past.

No one moored at the float could relax once they saw the *Hobo* or heard it in operation. There was always the fear that I might choose one of them as my target for mooring beside. All the other boat owners were kept alert once I became a boat owner. No one really dared spend too much time away from their boat as that young idiot with the *Hobo* might decide to make his daily trial run and then return for a crash landing while attempting to moor beside them. Everyone had to stand by with a pole to fend me off if necessary as I drifted past.

Now the day of a real maiden voyage had finally arrived. I had made several short ten minute circles around in the harbor getting acquainted with both my steering at the stern and also learning to sprint back to the rudder post once the engine started and then the reverse, sprint back to claw at the battery to stop the engine and discontinue its momentum, hopefully.

I advised Bill and Mike of our venture, promising them it would not be necessary for them to bail during the trip, as I had replaced the old hand pump that drew the bilge water out onto the deck with a new plunger I had molded from an old boot. The new plunger fit fairly snugly, so it could be pumped up and down regularly drawing up a boot full of bilge water each stroke to be unloaded back into the bay.

Bright and early the following day we untied from the float and turned the bow of the *Hobo* in the right direction to leave the float. Noticeably, every other boat owner was out on deck observing our departure with a long pole handy in case of mishaps. I twisted over the flywheel after priming and the engine sprang to life with Bill at the stern controlling the rudder and Mike standing up so he could watch where we were going. I remained inside watching where we had been, and keeping an eye on the engine so it could be stopped if need be in an emergency, such as meeting another boater foolish enough to be out on the water at the same time as the *Hobo*. I could only watch Bill's expression to tell if an emergency was appearing or not, as the noise from the engine made small talk impossible.

All appeared well, as Bill had not yet yelled to stop. In fact he was nodding that all was going well, so I took a chance and went out on deck to see our progress. Bill was depending on Mike to assure him that he was heading in the right direction as there was a blind spot of about 180 degrees magnitude looking forward from the rudder post. The only way for the rudder operator to get a view of what lay ahead was to turn the *Hobo* sideways momentarily to look, then return to the real course. This of course caused any other boats traveling in the vicinity to be on the alert, as it was impossible for them to guess the actual direction we were headed.

We had fair tide and were traveling fairly well even at slow speed, as the tide was flooding at probably four knots an hour. Once we were clear of all docks and permanent structures I decided to give the *Hobo* full power by advancing the timer at the engine. I had never had the opportunity to do this before when surrounded by docks and moored boats. Once I advanced the timer the engine immediately revved up much faster, and the boat began vibrating, as if it was having a fit of some kind. Frightened, I again slowed it down until the worst of the vibrations had ceased. We decided this would be our cruising speed for the remainder of the trip.

Putt-putting along we were soon passing Scow Bay, a small settlement about three miles south of Petersburg. It was comforting to know that if anything happened we could tow the *Hobo* with the skiff to a mooring float in Scow Bay where we had friends.

We swept on past Scow Bay with the fair tide pushing us along. Tonka Point was our next landfall up ahead and I, for one, began to get the feeling I was another Christopher Columbus and we were headed on a voyage of adventure and discovery of new lands. How my companions felt, I never asked as it was difficult to shout to each other above the loud putt-putt of the exhaust which kept enveloping the three of us in steam each time it was necessary for the helmsman to turn us sideways to see where the hell we were headed. Papke's place was our goal.

Papke was an old bachelor who lived in a tiny shack about ten miles from town. There he grew a garden of most everything possible, and occasionally rowed all the way to town to sell his boxes of strawberries and, later in the season his raspberries. The stove on the *Hobo* was still inoperative but we did have enough sense to each have an apple to munch on, so food was not a problem yet.

Once past Tonka Point, we had several channel markers to avoid. They were each constructed of several pilings driven into the bottom of the channel, then strapped tightly together at their top, with a kerosene light of either red or green attached to show which side to pass each on in mid-channel.

Once we had safely avoided all of these, we turned to putt-putt up in front of Papke's where we stopped and dropped our anchor. The anchor did not have sufficient line to reach bottom, however, and we had to haul it back again by hand. I once again started our engine and propelled us closer to Papke's until we could readily see the bottom, and drop our anchor again.

We had no plans for a long visit so were

sure we would once again be under way on our return trip long before the tide went out and left us high and dry. Once the *Hobo* was anchored, we all piled into the skiff and rowed ashore, including my dog, Kamoke. He had spent most of the voyage up at the bow where it was quieter and there was just enough room for him to lay down. It was his first experience on a motor boat and I could see he was not enjoying it one bit. He had always before been able to either get up forward in the bow of our skiff while I rowed, so he could watch the beaches for ducks, bear, or deer at which he would growl, or else he could lay down on the stern seat and sleep peacefully while I rowed on and on. He did not appreciate this noisy new boat we now had.

Anyway, we landed on Papke's beach, tied up our skiff, then walked up to visit him only to discover he still wasn't awake and up, as he usually read by lantern or wrote in his diary until daybreak summer or winter. We all wandered down the beach for an hour or so until we saw smoke coming from his chimney. Then knocked on his tiny door until he opened it and stood looking out at the three of us and the dog.

We were all invited inside which was quite a problem because there was really only room for Papke himself inside. His wood block for chopping wood sat directly in the middle of his tiny shack making it possible for him to lay in his bunk and cut wood with his axe and then stoke his stove without ever getting up. Nevertheless, he insisted we all come in, except my dog, who chose to remain outside anyway.

Papke got more water from his rainwater barrel so we could all have coffee with him. He also got biscuits for us which he kept beneath his pillow to discourage any mice from getting at them. Once the water was hot, he poured it through an old percolator that contained coffee grounds into three old empty coffee cans for us. He filled the only cup he owned, which was one of metal painted white, for himself.

It was necessary to drink the coffee black and it was terrible. He tore two biscuits in half so all four of us could have a half to munch on. He had no butter so it was necessary to chew on a dry slab of biscuit and try to wash it down with sips of black coffee from our coffee cans. We could only guess what he might have used these coffee cans for previously, as he was not one to travel far afield even to relieve himself.

Once I had swallowed the final part of my biscuit, I wanted to discard the remainder of my coffee even though I was terribly hungry. I finally managed to pour most of the remainder of my coffee in amongst Papke's split wood. From there it would, hopefully, trickle down onto his gravel floor and disappear from sight. I think Mike and Bill did likewise as they were attempting to rise to leave. This was difficult because Papke had his ceiling beams loaded with vegetables he had dried for winter use. In addition he had exotic plants hanging down to within a couple feet of the floor.

We finally managed to bid Papke adieu, which wasn't easy because he loved to have company and would talk on and on without stopping for a deep breath when he had a captive audience. He followed us down to our skiff, never missing one sentence. He continued to shout additional information across the water until we had our anchor hauled back and started our engine. The engine drowned out anymore of Papke's recitation of experience with his plants and problems with crows, ravens, robins, deer, etc. We all waved and he waved back, and we were on our way back to Petersburg.

We had stayed longer than planned as we could see the sun was now setting, which meant it was six or seven p.m. We had no navigation lights on the *Hobo,* so must try to return to Petersburg before dark. This was not to be, although we had fair tide for our return trip as the tide was now ebbing, darkness still found us just passing Scow Bay and probably invisible to everyone except for the noise and steam we were producing as we went past.

Now our navigating became sticky as we were soon being propelled past the docks. The strong outgoing tide made it very difficult to turn out of the tide and into the main harbor, where a strong back eddy was no doubt running in the opposite direction to compensate for the outflowing current.

Once we entered the boat harbor it was apparent we were now going every bit as fast in the opposite direction with moored boats everywhere for us to dodge. I immediately stopped the motor to slow down our forward progress, but the tide continued to sweep us on past moored boat after moored boat with no prospects of even lassoing one. Fortunately, most of the owners of the occupied boats had not heard our approach, because I had stopped the engine well away from the moorage.

Now straight ahead, Bob Allen's machine shop and foundry appeared. The foundry was the first obstacle in our way that could prevent us from continuing right on under the dock and out the other side, if we were fortunate enough to miss the dock piling. This, however, was not to be, as we came to a stop with a loud crash as the bow of the *Hobo* smashed into Bob Allen's foundry building and damn near ended up in his forge.

Once stopped we all three began immediately pushing desperately to disengage ourselves from his building and get the hell away from it. Luckily he had built a home uptown and did not now reside upstairs in the building. Even with all three of us struggling to push ourselves and the *Hobo* away, we seemed glued to his building. What had become of Kamoke in the dark, I had not a clue, but he had been sleeping in daylight directly up on the bow where we were now all three pushing as hard as possible to escape the wrath of Bob Allen if he had possibly heard our crash landing.

Still unable to disengage ourselves, we stopped

for a further look at our predicament and then realized it was our damned anchor that was keeping us locked tightly to Bob Allen's foundry in a mating position. The anchor which protruded over the bow had gone inside the building. Then the flukes had dropped down and were holding us fast. With no hopes of disengaging ourselves in the dark, it seemed only sensible to cut the damned anchor loose so we could escape. Luckily Mike had a pocketknife, so we were able to cut the line by sawing through it, and then quietly pull ourselves back by hand along the moored boats, to a moorage as far away as possible from his building.

Once we were tied up snugly, we quietly strolled back again to the foundry shed. We discovered the door was open making it possible to retrieve the damned anchor and carry it back to the *Hobo*. How we ever managed to get away with colliding with the foundry building without waking up half the town, I'll never know. Although in later years I often had machine work done at Bob Allen's scow, I never admitted to him that I was the one who left the gaping hole in the back wall of his foundry.

As for my dog, Kamoke, it would have been an interesting tale if he had been able to tell us how the hell he avoided getting hurt when the bow of the *Hobo* crashed into that building with him apparently up there in harm's way.

Now with the maiden voyage completed, I

made plans to prepare for the fishing season by moving aboard the *Hobo* and getting the wood stove operating to keep warm and to be able to cook fish if nothing else was available.

One bunk had previously been used directly beside the engine. This bunk I intended to share with my dog, but it was so difficult for him to crawl across the engine to get into the bunk that he chose instead to sleep on the bench that held the stove. Perhaps he had already decided he wanted a clear avenue of escape after the one experience with Bob Allen's building. However, I soon realized he had other motives. He wasn't about to over-sleep in a leaky boat that might fill up with water and sink. He wanted to be out where he was aware of how much water was coming in. After three or four hours without pumping, the water would eventually rise over the floor.

I'm sure I had the first automatic bilge alarm in Petersburg, thirty years before anyone else. Kamoke would only doze until he spotted water on the floor. Then he would immediately start whining and scratching at the closed door. This, of course, awakened me to let him out and forced me to pump the bilge dry before returning again to my bunk.

I was still rather flushed with importance after our successful voyage to and from Papke's, even though there had been a few minor difficulties on the trip, such as crashing into and partially demolishing the foundry building. Although we had no accurate timepieces during our voyage, we had all three agreed we had made the trip to Papke's in each direction averaging easily seven knots with fair tide helping drive us along. Therefore, our trip had taken only one and a half hours each way, Petersburg to Papke's then Papke's to Petersburg on return. When I delightedly informed one of the older fisherman at the float the following day of our successful trip and the time it had taken to do so, he gave me the ultimate, humiliating put-down. "Your clock must have stopped," he said.

Hoping to perhaps get a bit more respect as a boat owner if my boat was repainted, I invested in another gallon of tar and smeared it onto the decks. They had become bare from constant swamping with each tide. Not knowing it is necessary to mix some type of drying mixture with tar for it to eventually set up, I soon discovered that my newly tarred decks were a skating rink for both myself and Kamoke. For me it was only inconvenient, as the tar would wear off somewhat when I got on solid footing on the float, and didn't bother me once I removed my boots and crawled into the bunk. For poor Kamoke, it was another story, because the tar stuck to his paws making it necessary for him to constantly lick at his feet hoping to remove the sticky tar that no doubt burned him miserably.

He would trot a few feet behind me on the float, then sit down and lick at his burning paws allowing me to get perhaps a hundred yards ahead. He would then have to give up and run to catch up with me, then again sit down and commence licking the tar off his paws. This was a little bit embarrassing for me, as it did slow our progress uptown with him stopping every few feet to examine his paws. More distracting was his constant trotting up and down across our newly tarred decks while I tried to sleep inside. I would yell at him, "Stop trotting, dammit," and the poor dog would do his best to stop and be quiet. But, within moments his poor feet would start burning again and only constant trotting up and down with short stops to try and remove the tar from his feet would quiet him.

Kamoke and I fished the remainder of the salmon season with the Hobo, utilizing it as a towboat for moving ourselves to better producing areas as the season progressed, where we would then commence gillnetting with our large net skiff, leaving Hobo at anchor till needed.

With school commencing immediately after Labor Day it was necessary to look for permanent moorage for winter for the *Hobo*, preferably where it would remain out of water safely to avoid pumping every four hours night and day. On one of our final trips across Wrangell Narrows before school began, we passed a fellow obviously in difficulty rowing against the strong outflowing ebb tide. Slowing down as slow as possible, I offered to tow him safely across the narrows to his moorage near his home. It was obvious his main problem was from consuming too much liquor in Petersburg before attempting to row himself against the tide.

He agreed to being towed and threw us his tie-up line at the bow of his skiff, nearly falling flat in the bottom of his skiff in the process. We tied his skiff up to the Hobo securely, restarted the engine, then towed him slowly behind till we reached the opposite shore near his own moorage, then released him with his line to row the final few feet on his own. I had stopped our engine to avoid his careening on ahead while we released the skiff as he was not in the best condition to navigate his own boat safely. He thanked us over and over for the tow, then inquired what I planned to do with the *Hobo* when I returned to school. I admitted a had no firm plans and was still looking for a safe storage area, preferably at high tide mark where the Hobo would be out of the water most of the time.

"Why not sell it to me?" he asked, "I'll give you $75 cash for it right now!"

"Let me think about it overnight," I said. "I'll give you my answer tomorrow."

"Okay," he said. "I'll be home tomorrow."

I slept little all that night, weighing the opportunity of making three times the original cost of the *Hobo* against the problem of also pumping after school each evening to keep it afloat. The profit of the sale won me over, naturally, and the following day Kamoke and

I took our final voyage with the *Hobo* across Wrangell Narrows and tied it securely to the float near the new owner's home. It was for us a sad day as I had earlier removed my clothing and rifle and also swept up the floor. Kamoke, too, seemed to sense something was changing as he trotted back and forth steadily now that the tarred decks had finally dried into a shiny surface!

We walked up the trail to the buyer's home where a home brew party was apparently in progress and everyone was in high spirits. I told him I was accepting his offer of $75 for sale of the *Hobo* and would also be happy to show him how to start and operate the boat. He assured me it would be no problem as he had previously owned a similar engine. I also offered to demonstrate how the manual hand pump operated, as the *Hobo* did leak a little. He assured me that would be no problem either and he had used and repaired uncounted hand pumps also. Only the formality of counting out $75 cash and our solemn handshake with each other remained, and that was quickly completed. Kamoke and I departed to row back across Wrangell Narrow in our gillnet skiff.

Obviously his understanding of a boat leaking a "little" and my interpretation of a "little" leak were far different. He did not come down his trail to view his purchase until the following day when only the tip of the mast of the *Hobo* remained visible above water! He was able later to salvage the engine but never did have the luxury of a ride on his acquisition!

As for Kamoke and I, we went on to other boats as the years went by, gradually getting larger and better ones each time!

11 *"The seas were now breaking completely across their trap frame and had washed their trap watchman's cabin loose. They helplessly watched as it floated away. Soon they had to turn back to keep their own boat safe."*

The Fish Trap That Failed

Fish traps were not unique to Alaska. Similar structures had been used, probably for centuries, both in Asia and Europe. Once people immigrated from Europe to the Atlantic Coast, it was not long before these same types of structures for trapping migrating fish were erected along the coastline of this continent. The early traps were on poles with webbing at various angles to confuse the fish and entice them into a final encircled section, from which they could be easily removed.

The Alaska Indians used similar pole fences, or rock fences where poles were not available, to divert the salmon schools that drifted back and forth with flood and ebb tide from upstream back again to salt water, until they had once again adapted to fresh water and could swim upstream to spawn. Indian fish traps had no section for entrapping the salmon. Instead they relied on the tide. When the water dropped away with ebb tide, the Indians would drive the salmon behind these fences and capture them. They would then smoke and dry them beside the streams on racks.

The White Man also began his salmon fishing near the streams, where the salmon were schooled tightly together. This made it a simple matter to encircle them with their seines and nets for delivery to the canneries that were springing up all over Southeastern Alaska in the early 1900s. Soon it became obvious there were not enough sockeye streams to accommodate the expanding fishing fleets hoping to join in the harvest at the stream mouth.

Thus began the experiments with pile traps. This type of trap was stretched out from shore on piling driven into the sea bottom with a pile driver. Wire fences were strung and fastened to the piling that ran out from shore for hundreds of feet. Then compartments of wire were placed to divert the salmon schools into the final enclosures. The final enclosure was made of web and was called a spiller.

These pile traps worked very well in areas where the current would set the salmon schools into the wire fence, or lead as it was named, and then divert the salmon along the lead until they entered the final structure. Once in the final structure, they swam along through large inviting entrances that narrowed down to very small escape routes until there was no turning back.

Pile traps had two faults. They could only be located where there was a shallow shore-line running offshore for hundreds of feet so soon most of the suitable areas were taken up by salmon canneries. Secondly, winter storms and marine growth usually destroyed any structure left standing over winter, so pile driving equipment was necessary to place pile traps on location each year.

This limited the number of trap sites available until more experimenting was done with anchored fish traps, or floating traps, as they were called. The Heckman brothers at Ketchikan were credited with perfecting a floating trap that fished as well as the pile traps.

These floating traps could be placed almost anywhere along the protected Southeastern Alaska shoreline, even where the water was extremely deep. Migrating salmon schools rarely swim deeper than a hundred feet. Therefore, a floating lead stretching out from shore, attached to floating logs, and stretching down from these floating logs to no more than one hundred feet, could divert salmon schools outward through confusing pens to the final enclosure where they would be entrapped. These structures could accommodate many thousands of salmon alive until brailed into scows or boats for delivery to the cannery.

Now began a new breed of entrepreneurs springing up to join in the fish trap bonanza. Floating traps could be constructed on a level, protected beach by individuals who could hand log their own spruce trees. These trees needed to be huge to provide sufficient buoyancy to float the trap, all the wire and web necessary to entrap salmon, plus a trap watchman's cabin.

Floating Fishtrap

The watchman's cabin was always to be occupied unless a storm forced the watchman ashore to a similar cabin, for safety.

Usually, a powerful tug was hired, plus a rigging scow, to anchor the floating trap into position once it had been towed to its location. To avoid this extra expense, some trap owners would pool their resources and tow their floating trap frames to location themselves, often utilizing two of their own boats.

Clyde Sheldon and two partners leased a trap site on Prince of Wales Island, which they were confident would fish well with a floating trap. They fell, then hand logged down into the salt water, several huge spruce trees. Then they towed the logs into a protected harbor that had a long, level beach, where they could float the logs into position and lash them together with cables to make their trap frame. It took most of one winter before their trap frame was ready to staple the wire mesh to, and finally install the webbing for their spiller. The spiller could be raised or lowered by windlass and hand power to remove the salmon as needed.

Their final task was to build anchors for anchoring their fish trap when they arrived at their trap site. First, they built four large wire mesh containers on the logs. One was positioned at each corner of the trap frame, so they could be loaded with several tons of rocks, and then rolled overboard. Next they carried huge boulders from the beach and rolled them into these wire containers. Naturally, these large wire stacks of rocks were almost awash, even with the calm weather in the harbor.

By the time they completed the anchors, the season opening was nearly at hand. They had not been able to locate another boat to help with towing their trap out to their site, so they elected to gamble and go it alone with their boat, *Collette*. The *Collette* could barely move their trap frame along at a mile an hour.

It took twenty-four hours of towing just to reach the entrance to Clarence Strait. Now they would need to tow their trap across several miles of unprotected water, which sometimes turned rough suddenly, if a wind sprang up.

A light breeze was blowing as they began towing out into the straits, but they had outgoing tide in their favor, so they continued on. They were almost to mid-channel when the tide turned against them and the wind increased. Now it was as far back to shelter as it would be to continue on across Clarence Strait to reach their trap site and shelter. The weather continued to worsen until it was obvious they were not even making headway against the wind and tide.

The seas were now breaking completely across their trap frame and had washed their trap watchman's cabin loose. They helplessly watched as it floated away. Soon they had to turn back to keep their own boat safe. Turning as slowly as possible in the seas, to reverse their course safely, they saw one of their boulder anchors wash overboard. It took the long anchor cable attached to the stack of boulders with it, which, of course, anchored one corner of their trap. It was now impossible to tow any farther. All they could do was release themselves from the trap and head to a safe harbor until the wind abated.

It was mid-afternoon the following day, before it calmed down enough for them to venture back out to their trap, which they hoped would be anchored, where they had abandoned it the previous day. However, during the storm, all three remaining anchors had washed overboard and had separated the corners of the trap frame from the cable lashings. Now there were four separate sections of logs anchored in the middle of Clarence Strait creating a menace to navigation. Not having any equipment to retrieve their heavy rock anchors, they could only cut the anchors loose from the logs and allow the logs to float to shore, hopefully, while they turned homeward to Wrangell in total disgust!

This type of disaster happened many, many times to a great many individuals hoping to enter the fish trap bonanza in the early 1900s. Heavily in debt to a bank or cannery for the equipment they had lost, they could only forfeit their trap site to repay their debts. In a few years, the majority of trap sites and traps were owned or controlled by a few corporations loosely banded together as the Canned Salmon Industry. The Industry was represented in Washington, D.C., by paid lobbyists, who could often exert pressure enough to get a bit of favoritism for the Industry for extended fishing time in poor producing areas. This stranglehold of the commercial salmon industry continued right up to statehood, when fish traps were abolished. Distrust of any federal control of Alaska's resources continues to this day with older residents, and rightfully so!

12

"Run, they did, these huge diesel engines, on and on with smoke rings belching out the exhaust, and little wavelettes running off and away from the sides of the tenders due to the tremendous vibrations they created."

Early Diesels and Smoke Rings

C annery tenders large enough and powerful enough to tow fish traps out to location and to tow the pile driver out to drive each season's pile traps were needed desperately in Southeastern Alaska in the 1920s and 30s. Originally, most tenders were powered with gasoline engines that used a low grade fuel called distillate, which was a mixture of today's diesel fuel and gasoline. These engines used a "make and break" ignition system which utilized an igniter for spark. The igniter was a coil and spring assembly that snapped in sequence with the piston to produce a big spark. However, distillate was explosive, and it often caused fires when the engines backfired.

The diesel engine was named for the German inventor Otto Diesel, who developed one of the first high compression engines that operated without spark plugs to ignite the fuel. There were some early diesel engines in Southeastern Alaska, called semi-diesels, that had red-hot cylinder heads so the diesel fuel could ignite and fire each time the piston came up to firing order. The semi-diesels needed a large, open engine room to allow the tremendous amount of heat from the cylinder heads to be dispelled into open air outside. They belched black soot and smoke, and colored the engineers likewise until diesel fuel was improved over the years.

Full diesel engines were as yet quite rare. Two of the first cannery tenders to be powered by a diesel engine were the *William T. Muir* and the *Yes Bay*. Both had a Metz and Weiss three-cylinder diesel engine with water-cooled cylinder heads. Both engines were "liberated" from captured German U-boats at the end of World War I, and were installed in the hull of the boats during construction.

These two engines had no clutch so had to be stopped to reverse the rotation of the engine. A compression release was necessary to allow the engineer to place a long metal bar in the proper hole drilled in the flywheel for setting the engine either in reverse or forward. On a signal from the pilothouse, the engineer would bar the flywheel over to a mark at top center, then set the flywheel back to another mark on the flywheel ten degrees before top center. This would put the engine in reverse. Likewise, another mark on the flywheel at ten degrees forward of top center would start the huge engine in forward. The compression release was reset to allow full compression, and the engine was given a shot

Diesel-powered Tender

of compressed air to start it revolving.

Signals were given to the engineer by the Captain in the pilothouse by bells, a loud gong similar to one used in a prize fighting ring, and another smaller bell similar to the ones on

Santa's Sleigh. With the engine in stopped position, one gong meant go ahead slowly. The engineer would immediately bar the flywheel over to forward position, and a big POOF blew a smoke ring out the exhaust as the engine commenced forging ahead at slow speed. Another gong was a signal to stop. So the engineer stopped the engine, released the compression, and barred the huge flywheel over to top center to wait for the following signal. If the gong was rung twice, it meant start up in reverse. The engine would chug slowly in reverse until another single gong sounded which meant stop the engine again and wait for another signal from the pilothouse. If again one gong was sounded, it meant go forward again, and if at that time a jingle on Santa's Sleigh bells was also given, it meant ahead full speed. Now, one gong following a full speed jingle would mean slow down until another gong was sounded to stop the engine and roll the flywheel to start position.

Naturally, this meant a tender powered with a direct reversible engine (no clutch) had to be handled rather carefully, with a pause between a signal from the pilothouse to the engine room, and another pause while the engineer on duty spotted the flywheel for forward or reverse, then shot the air to the engine and another huge POOF and smoke ring went out the exhaust.

The one signal the engineer did not want to hear while traveling forward at full speed, was four gongs and the jingle of sleigh bells. This was emergency full speed reverse and meant all hell had broken loose. It was impossible for even the fastest engineer to stop the engine, then reverse, in time to avoid plowing into a rock or anything else that suddenly appeared ahead of the boat.

Remarkably, there were very few accidents caused with all this complicated signaling. It was remarkable, because these diesel tenders always had either a fish scow alongside that they were maneuvering into the conveyor float to be unloaded of salmon, or a pile driver alongside being maneuvered into the dock. This type of signaling continued for many years until workable clutches were perfected that could withstand the tremendous torque of reversing a huge spinning propeller.

How the German U-boats could travel undetected in the Atlantic with smoke rings belching out the exhaust in daylight and sparks flying out the exhaust in the dark, is a good question. I think it must have been a pleasure to dive under water and power with a quiet battery so the noisy diesel could be stopped for a while.

It was necessary for tenders powered by direct reversible diesel engines to have a smaller gasoline powered stationary engine situated up forward on the fo'c'sle to power the winches. The winches were used to brail the salmon traps, because the main engines must remain stopped while the tender was moored alongside the fish trap. The winches lifted brailers full of salmon out of the fish trap and onto the salmon scow. It would be towed back to the cannery where the fish were processed.

Run, they did, these huge diesel engines, on and on with smoke rings belching out the exhaust, and little wavelettes running off and away from the sides of the tenders due to the tremendous vibrations they created.

13

"Each moment now Clyde's cannery was submerging more and more. The water was roaring past until it was impossible to even jump back on the cannery float and run up to phone Clyde to come...."

Tides and the Submerged Shrimp Cannery

Our local tides are always a source of wonder to visitors traveling through Southeastern Alaska. Here at Petersburg, a hundred miles from the ocean, a rise and fall of twenty-four feet, or four feet per hour is not uncommon. We are situated at Wrangell Narrows where the current rushes in at five to six miles per hour in some of the narrowest places. Then the tide reverses after flooding in for six hours and rushes out for another six hours at ebb. We will have a height of twenty feet at high flood, then a four foot minus at low, low ebb, or four foot below a normal low tide.

The piling driven to hold the floats in the harbor must be of additional length to allow for the extra rise and fall of the tides, because hundreds of boats are moored to these floats and rise and fall with each tide. To connect these floats to the shore itself, a ramp is connected firmly to shore with giant hinges. The ramp is also connected at the other end to the float with wheels running on a track that allow the ramp to rise and fall with the tide.

Shortly before World War II began for the United States, I was moored at our city float. When walking ashore, a group of Naval officers were standing at the bottom of the ramp in heated conversation. It was almost necessary to squeeze past several of them, all decked out with gold braid on their sleeves and caps. One called out, "Young man. What's happened here? A few hours ago this ramp was nearly level and now it is almost perpendicular. What's wrong?"

"The tide went out," I answered to a look of disbelief from the group. I hurried on up the steep ramp as I feared I was about to be held for a sanity hearing otherwise.

Another time, a Salvation Army officer asked me if there was a city ordinance against posting signs on our floats, and I replied that I had never heard of any restrictions. "Well, this morning I came down and put up several signs about a meeting this evening, but now they are all gone," he said.

"Where did you post them?" I asked.

"Right here on these big poles," he answered.

"Well, there they are," I said, pointing down underwater about three feet. "You have to tack them to the float itself, on the hand railings or some other likely place that remains afloat," I explained to an embarrassed young officer.

I often tied my boat at Clyde Sheldon's floating shrimp cannery which was only a short walk from my home. Clyde and I were good friends and had fished near each other for many years during the salmon season. In winter he operated his shrimp cannery when labor was available. I knew I was always welcome to moor at his plant to avoid the longer distance uptown to the city floats.

His cannery was moored to his own float which had a ramp for his employees to come and go from shore each day to hand-pick the shrimp. They worked in a picking room which contained tables and benches where they sat while removing the shells from the shrimp. His cannery building was erected on huge logs which allowed it to float a couple feet above the water for clearance from the wake of passing motorboats.

Over the years, however, the massive logs that floated his cannery had become water-logged and bug eaten by marine life, as do all untreated logs eventually. This honeycombing caused the logs to lose buoyancy. Each big minus tide, one of his old pilings that had been eaten away by marine life and toppled over, would resurface. This stump created a hazard to any boat moored directly above it, because, when the boat settled down on the minus tide, this stump could pierce up through the hull and sink the boat. I always made certain to moor carefully so I could never actually settle down on this snag, but even so, on dead low water, it appeared dangerously near.

Clyde had nearly sunk his own boat on the

same hazard, and we discussed the possibility of removing it someday. His plan was to first encircle the stump with a chain and attach several sticks of dynamite. Then he would move his entire shrimp cannery for a day or two and set-off the dynamite. He felt the explosion would create such a jar that the piling would spring loose from where it had been driven years earlier. The huge problem in this plan, which kept him from doing it, was moving the shrimp cannery for a day or two while blasting, since he hadn't done so for several years.

I was moored at his cannery one fall evening during extreme minus tides and stood by to make certain my boat remained well clear of this hazard. At low water this old snag appeared to stick a couple of feet out of the water. I thought it was an ideal time to try my solution to the problem.

I unshackled my anchor from my anchor chain, so I could utilize the chain itself. I wrapped it tightly around and around the stump of piling that showed above low water. Then I lashed my chain solidly to a large cleat on the corner of the cannery which was used to moor the cannery to a good piling. Darkness was coming on, and it was dinner time at home, so I hurried home, planning to return as quickly as possible.

I gulped down dinner as quickly as possible and returned to the floating cannery only to discover that it was now starting to submerge with the roaring flood tide. In fact, I had to creep around the upper end of the cannery where the boiler and canning machinery was located to even get aboard my boat.

I hadn't been gone more than one hour, but the tide had already flooded back in probably two or three feet. It was getting impossible to even get in the vicinity of where I had fastened my chain to his float. I now realized the folly of using my chain. Now with the tide rushing past, I couldn't even chop my chain loose with an axe, as I could possibly have done if I had used a line rather than a chain.

Each moment now Clyde's cannery was submerging more and more. The water was roaring past until it was impossible to even jump back on the cannery float and run up to phone Clyde to come running. "Dear, God, what shall I do," I asked myself. Now the water was almost up to the window in the picking room and I could hear all kinds of crashing going on inside in the dark. In a very few minutes now, the water would be rushing completely over the entire structure, submerging all the machinery also.

"Clyde is going to kill me," I kept telling myself, now sick with shame at what a stupid thing I had done. Even my boat was beginning to list over, as my lines tightened on the cleat underwater. I slacked off my stern line, then ran up to the bow hoping to do likewise there before I listed anymore.

Just as I reached down to slack my bowline,

the whole floating cannery seemed to spring upwards like a German U-Boat surfacing and, "Thank God," once again Clyde had a cannery afloat. I was sure the boiler and other machinery had probably also been submerged, but could not tell as it was pitch dark. With a flashlight, I could now unhitch my chain from the old snag, that had pulled completely out of its hole and was bouncing in the tide, held fast by my chain.

What a relief, when my chain was unfastened, to see the troublesome old stump piling go bouncing along down Wrangell Narrows to its final resting place, wherever that might be. I was shaking so badly with relief that I had trouble stumbling home, but I was too ashamed to phone Clyde until daylight came and I had a chance to view the damage to his cannery.

Daylight didn't come until nearly eight a.m and Clyde arrived himself to enter the cannery and switch on the boiler. It immediately roared to life leaving me shaking with disbelief and relief. Now the pickers were arriving also and everyone was dismayed to discover all the picking tables and benches were piled in a heap against the wall which had stopped them from floating any farther. Seaweed was also on the floor and some was even up on the windowsills.

Once Clyde had the boiler going to heat water for cooking the shrimp, he came outside to investigate. He could see no actual damage except for the mess inside the picking room.

I stood by on the sidelines, not offering any

opinion about what might have happened, waiting for Clyde to discover for himself what must have happened. Fortunately, he decided that somehow his mooring cable had become entangled in the old snag, and had eventually torn it out of its lodging after part of the cannery became submerged. I nodded in relief that he was no doubt correct. If he had other doubts, he never spoke of them, and I certainly wasn't one to argue with his decision.

"All's well that ends well," they say!

Part 4

Are We Having Fun Yet?

Salvation Army Days

Politicians and the Water Pitcher

The Girls of Warm Springs Bay

*Port Alexander: Fishing and the
Fourth of July*

14 *"When the Lassie reappeared, we would ... march to the Salvation Army Hall, with John Oscar quietly setting the pace on his drum. It was now nearing eight p.m. and, at that time, the bell at the town hall would ring announcing curfew, which scattered us kids homeward...."*

Salvation Army Days

B OOM! BOOM!...... BOOM! BOOM! BOOM! Each night at seven p.m. John Oscar Harris, a full-blooded Alaskan Indian, would stand outside the Salvation Army Hall and beat on his bass drum. The drum was strapped in a harness over his shoulders to distribute its weight. It was a huge drum which nearly touched the ground when John strode along with it, amidst the marching group headed down Sing Lee Alley to town center. The drum's weight was no problem for John Oscar who, as a young man, had carried supplies up the Chilkoot Trail during the 1898 Gold Rush to the Klondike, for which he was paid fifty cents a pound.

He never tired of telling us kids how he would have a cast iron stove weighing more than one hundred pounds strapped onto his back, then have a fifty pound sack of flour placed into the oven of the stove. He then took his place in the human chain of packers struggling up an almost vertical hill. The packers climbed side by side with horses staggering under loads that often made them collapse.

Now, he was in his sunset years and intensely proud to be selected as the one to summon the people to the meetings at the Salvation Army Hall, and to walk at the rear of the parade beating his drum in unison to the pace of the march.

Although the faithful followers of the Salvation Army in Petersburg were all Indians, the Salvation Army Captain, his wife, and two Army Lassies were white. They conducted the meetings and prayers and had a big pot of hot soup available daily at noon to feed any hungry Indian children who attended school.

Seven days each week were devoted to helping the Indians and trying to improve their circumstances, while the Indians tried to adapt to the White Man's system. The Indian culture had lived on the bountiful resources of Southeastern Alaska, sharing with each other, with no need to save, as there was always more available. Now they were leaving their villages to come to the White Man's World, to work for him, and to earn money to buy food in tin cans. It was a totally alien system where individuals saved for themselves and did not share with the community.

In this strange new environment, it was small wonder that many Indians tried to find comfort and escape with bootleg alcohol. Alcohol gave them a lift, momentarily, and allowed them to forget for the moment that only their labor was welcome. Even the White Man's school was not open to the Indian children.

We smart aleck kids would hear John Oscar beating on the drum and rush down to be in front of the Army Hall when the parade was being assembled. The regular group of Army members would all take their places in line with the Salvation Army Lassies and the Captain in their uniforms at the front of the parade.

We kids were permitted to join in the march if we remained orderly during the march and joined in when the parade stopped for prayer and song. Once the line of marchers started off, we kids would swing into step

"Smart aleck" kids

directly behind John Oscar and his drum, at the rear of the parade, immediately strutting out in our exaggerated German Army goose step we had seen in some news reels. We marched silently, except for the quiet, even beat of John Oscar's drum.

Some in the parade had likely been laying drunk in the gutter the previous night exactly where we now marched, but had somehow sobered up, cleaned up, eaten some hot soup at the Salvation Army Hall, and now marched proudly in their respective positions in our parade. No matter how drunk and foolish they may have been, they were always forgiven and accepted back into the fold.

When we reached the street light that illuminated both Jim Brennan's card room and also Wheeler's Drug Store, we stopped marching. The officers formed everyone into a large circle, and one of the Lassies would step forward, to the center of the circle, to give a short sermon to our group and anyone else on the street who might have stopped. The onlookers listened in respect, often removing their hats. Once the sermon was completed the Captain would usually step forward with his trumpet to give a small bit of trumpet playing to start the rest of us singing. I distinctly remember we would all sing out, "When the Roll is Called Up Yonder," at the top of our voices.

While we were all belting out this song, one of the Lassies would enter Jim Brennan's card room holding her tambourine out ahead of her for anyone of the onlookers who might have received a slight nudge of good will from her sermon. Passing around to the different card tables she would receive a fifty cent piece from the card dealer at each table; Poker Ole at the poker table, Johnny the Bunk at the rummy game table, and Johnny the Slick at the pinochle table.

Moving along, she would then circle the remainder of the card room, where the kibitzers were sitting on wooden benches swapping lies with each other. Most were like permanent fixtures, as they spent most of their time at the card room, which was warmed by a huge coal burning heater, under which Jim Brennan's dog, Dempsey, lay sleeping. Occasionally, during his wildest dreams, Dempsey would let a fart, and the card room would empty while both front and back doors were opened to air out the room. This was probably the only time of day many of the occupants got a breath of fresh air.

On returning towards the entrance again through the solid fog of cigar and cigarette smoke, she would pass near Jim Brennan, who sat near the door beside his big brass cash register. Always dressed up with a Celluloid collar, starched shirt, bow tie, suspenders, elastic cuff links, and blue serge pants, he looked exactly the very same as he had the last day of legal saloons ten years earlier. When the Lassie would re-appear out of the tobacco smoke, headed back for the entrance, Jim would ring open his cash register, and step down to hand her his fifty cent piece with a big flourish. The Lassie curtsied in return, which always made him beam for hours afterward.

When the Lassie came back out of Jim Brennan's, we would again form into a parade and march on through main street to the other card room of Charley Mann's. Here, again, we would form another circle and have one of the Lassies again step into the center to give another short sermon. Again the Captain would commence to play his trumpet to the tune of "In the Sweet By and By, We Will Meet by That Beautiful Shore," and the rest of us would join in singing at the top of our voices so all would hear. The Lassie would enter Charley Mann's with her tambourine outstretched for any donations she might receive, while circling more card tables amidst more tobacco smoke.

Charley Mann had an annual calendar he distributed to everyone in town. His card room adjoined the Bank of Petersburg, which each year proudly printed the amount of its assets, which usually showed a million dollars in deposits. This prompted Charley Mann to add at the bottom of his calendar, "My assets near one million dollars."

When the Lassie again appeared, we would cease our singing and again line-up for the return march to the Salvation Army Hall, with John Oscar quietly setting the pace on his drum. It was now nearing eight p.m. and, at that time, the bell at the town hall would ring announcing curfew, which scattered us kids homeward to avoid a lecture from the local police for being out on the street after curfew. Whether these occasional marches with the regular group of devoted improved our lives is difficult to say, but for sure it made us more tolerant of others. We learned tolerance by marching side by side with many who had gotten up out of the gutter to take their place in line and join us in song.

Those that returned to the Salvation Army Hall to disband were all treated to a hot bowl of soup, which was waiting for them on their arrival. This, I am sure, was quite likely the only good meal of the day for many of the Indians who were part of the flock.

15 *"The delegate to Congress, or a candidate seeking the position, would always speak first, droning on and on with an occasional stop to pour himself a glass of water from an enormous pitcher, to lubricate his throat."*

Politicians and the Water Pitcher

Once again elections are drawing near in Alaska and potential candidates are jockeying for publicity. It brings back memories of years gone by when Alaska was a territory and our governor was appointed by the President and his party.

Our only elected representative to Washington, D.C., was our delegate to Congress, who could not vote and could only speak to members of Congress when requested to do so. He had about as much real influence as a bucket of warm spit, as John Nance Garner once said of his own capacity as Vice President.

Candidates for territorial office in District I (Southeastern Alaska) would arrive by steamer with the delegate to Congress, and signs would hurriedly be placed all over town announcing their arrival in Petersburg. They would rent Enge's theater for the evening, promising a "Free Show" immediately following their speeches.

This, of course, would bring out practically the entire population, including all the kids, eager for a free show. People would stumble down Sing Lee Alley with flashlights, as it was poorly lit with street lights. Even Bob Kechison, proprietor of the Arctic Card Room, would limp on his cane to the theater with his dog, Kamoke, at his side.

Kamoke was allowed into the theater, for adult admission, and he always sat quietly beside his master, even when the kids were creating bedlam before a show. During a movie he watched the screen intently, occasionally sharing a Hershey bar with Bob.

Just before eight p.m. Mr. Enge would make the rounds of the theater to check the radiators which lined each side. Sometimes air locks caused the pipes to clank loudly and frighten the audience. He stopped at each radiator to drain off a bit of water and steam to relieve any air lock, then gave each radiator a wallop with a hammer.

Once these chores were completed, some prominent citizen of town would walk out with the candidates and introduce them one by one, to applause. Prior to 1942, District I had two senators and four representatives in the Alaska Territorial Legislature.

The delegate to Congress, or a candidate seeking the position, would always speak first, droning on and on with an occasional stop to pour himself a glass of water from an enormous pitcher, to lubricate his throat. It seemed to us kids he would never end, but finally he would turn to a candidate for senator and give him the floor. This gentleman would then go on and on, giving his qualifications plus drinking his share of water. Finally, about nine p.m., he would give the floor to a candidate for representative.

By now the water pitcher was getting nearly empty and all of us kids were squirming and muttering to each other, wondering how much longer they would continue. Even grown-ups were looking around the theater by now to see who would be the first to walk out. Several had already fallen asleep.

Finally, this candidate would run out of air and give the floor to the last speaker, who would nervously pour himself the last glass of water from the pitcher before beginning to talk. This pause was enough of an excuse for many in the audience to get up and slip out. As he began speaking, his audience was mostly empty seats with several rows of disgusted kids glaring at him impatiently.

The only one still listening intently was Kamoke, as his master had long before fallen asleep. The speaker would finally finish and sit down again, and our local citizen would announce the completion of the speeches to a small ripple of applause from the survivors in the audience.

The candidates would file off the stage and the theater would darken to excited whistles from the kids. Then a Mack Sennett comedy would come on the screen and run for fifteen minutes.

We kids realized our high hopes for a full feature movie as the price for enduring all the speeches was not to be. We filed out of the theater past the candidates greeting all the grown-ups at the front door and shaking their hands. Their popularity with us at this moment wouldn't have gotten them elected territorial dog catcher.

However, we had learned a valuable lesson in politics. The more important the candidate the more water he is entitled to take from the pitcher, with low man on the totem pole getting the least.

16

"Immediately upon being notified of the crisis, their boyfriends stopped work and also took off back up the same trail towards the girls' cabins, leaving the mill owner to just sit amidst all the lumber shaking his head in disbelief!"

The Girls of Warm Springs Bay

B aranof Hot Springs, or Warm Springs Bay as it is locally known, woke up one May day in 1927 to the electrifying news of Charles Lindbergh's nonstop solo flight across the Atlantic in his plane, the *Spirit of St. Louis.* This was a proud day for all Americans, for ours was the first country to accomplish this feat. Charley Johnson, nicknamed the Swede, had heard the news on his Atwater Kent radio, which was the only radio in Warm Springs Bay. Charley was, of course, ecstatic because he insisted Lindbergh was a Swede. No matter that Lindbergh was actually an American of Swedish descent, to Charley, a Swede was always a Swede no matter how many generations they had resided elsewhere.

Charley had been up since early morning waiting out in front of the bathhouse with this fabulous news to announce to everyone as they arrived. By mid-day everyone in Warm Springs Bay was gathered in front of the bathhouse discussing the great event. Even the hookers had come down the walk from their own establishments up on the hill to hear if the news was authentic.

One of the hookers to arrive was Petersburg Kate. She had acquired her nickname many years earlier when she had used her physical attributes to save the town from a fire that started in Jim Brennan's Saloon. She plopped her ample rear end down to dam up a small stream, allowing it to back up into a pool from which the fire fighters filled their buckets to douse the fire.

Halibut Emma was also among the celebrants from Hooker Hill who had come to join in the festivities. She had been so nicknamed it was said because she had contours similar to her namesake. Then there was Chippy Mary from the hill. The other hookers were not too friendly with her usually. She received her nickname from coming to visit her competitors when they had "guests" and doing her best to solicit their business for her establishment.

Anyway, for this day, all the "girls" forgot their differences to join in the celebration. Petersburg Kate invited everyone to stop in at her place for a free drink if they were in the neighborhood, and Halibut Emma did likewise, probably as a public relations effort. However, Chippy Mary only grunted that the other two "girls" had gotten carried away with the festivities. All in all it was a great day for Warm Springs Bay, and I'm sure even Lucky Lindy would have enjoyed it. The only thing that could destroy a celebration like this would be to see the boat *Valkyrie* come steaming into Warm Springs Bay with a group of Prohibition agents aboard. The moment the lines touched the float, the Prohibition agents would immediately disperse and commence raiding every establishment in the village searching for illegal liquor. The *Valkyrie* had arrived at five a.m. the previous year and the Prohi agents had raided and arrested two sporting houses where the "girls" had neglected to cache their liquor before retiring after the evening's work.

To be reasonably sure it wouldn't happen and surprise them again, each hooker had paid the local storekeeper to issue me one Hershey bar daily to watch out towards the entrance to Warm Springs Bay for the possible return of the *Valkyrie*. If that should occur, I was to immediately run up the hill pounding on their doors to alert them to the arrival of the Prohis.

This was a satisfactory arrangement for me, as it allowed me almost an unlimited amount of Hershey bars, if I was so inclined, or I could also use that credit at the store to take chances on the punch board in hopes of winning the .22 rifle which was one of the prizes. Also it kept me alert and up at near daybreak each morning all summer watching every boat that turned into Warm Springs Bay. The *Valkyrie* was easily identifiable as it was long and low with steam coming out the stern from the exhaust, and it had a green hull and white cabin. Although it did arrive several times that summer, no one was ever caught with liquor on their premises.

The mailboat *Estebeth* arrived once weekly with mail and freight plus any passengers who had come for the curative properties of the hot springs. My dog, Kamoke, and I always rushed down to meet the mailboat too, because there was little excitement in Warm Springs other than the arrival of an occasional visiting boat.

On this particular day when the mailboat arrived, I spotted a large gentleman preparing to step off in Warm Springs during the mailboat's four-hour layover each trip. I was positive I had seen him during the previous winter in Petersburg where he had recently arrived as the US Marshal to replace the retiring Marshal MacGregor.

I immediately took off up the plank walk to warn the "girls" about a US Marshal's arrival in Warm Springs with a reputation that he would arrest his own mother if he caught her with a drink of whiskey in her hand. Each hooker I alerted told me to run across the cable suspension bridge that crossed above the waterfall and advise her boyfriend about the crisis. After alerting each house about the US Marshal's arrival, I took off across the suspension bridge to the sawmill that was powered by the waterfall. Immediately upon being notified of the crisis, their boyfriends stopped work and also took off back up the same trail towards the girls' cabins, leaving the mill owner to just sit amidst all the lumber shaking his head in disbelief!

I then wandered innocently back across the bridge and back down to the store, passing this man as he stopped at each "girl's" cabin to knock and wait for someone to open the door

Warm Springs in 1927

for him. "AHA," this only confirmed my suspicion that he had traveled incognito by mailboat rather than on the *Valkyrie* to surprise them.

After knocking at every cabin and receiving no reply, he came back down the plank walk carrying his briefcase and stopped in at the store to talk to the proprietor, Harry Raymond, who sat most of the time with a drink of moonshine within his reach. Peeking into the store, I was startled to see Harry reach down under the counter and bring out his gallon container of moonshine. He poured a drink for himself and then one for the marshal.

I was horrified and immediately entered the store, walked directly back into the Post Office where Mrs. Raymond was busy distributing the mail, and told her Mr. Raymond had just poured a drink of moonshine for the Petersburg marshal. She looked puzzled for a minute then commenced laughing and shouted out to the two men sipping their drinks, "Here's the reason none of the girls are at home, Dick. Jackie alerted all of them that you're the marshal from Petersburg."

He looked startled for a moment and then he too began laughing. He told me I was mistaken as he was actually the Oregon Woolen Mills salesman that visited each year and took orders for sweaters and skirts from the "girls." He also said he had been mistaken before for Marshal Brown, and he had heard they had a strong resemblance.

I was stunned, of course, at this development for I had been complimented so often by all the "girls" for my alertness that I considered myself infallible. Now I must go back up the hill and on out on the muskeg to a lily pond where the "girls" and their boyfriends were probably hiding out.

However, when I arrived at their hiding place, it was to discover they were all having a great time. A nice fire was going beside the pond with Halibut Emma and her boyfriend making coffee and sandwiches while Chippy Mary and Petersburg Kate were both splashing around stark naked with their boyfriends in the lily pond. They did try to cover up their privates when they realized I was in their midst, by using lily pads front and rear. However, when I told them of the awful mistake I had made and how bad I felt, they would have none of it. They said they were having a great holiday and for me to go on back to the village and get my allotment of Hershey bars for the day.

The mailboat *Estebeth* was just untying when I returned to the dock and the Oregon Woolen Mills salesman was feeling no pain whatever after visiting with Harry Raymond and his moonshine that afternoon. He was out on the bow of the boat waving his hat good-bye to all as they chugged away.

17

By the time round two began inside the ring, all attention was riveted on the fights outside the ring that were more intense and weren't stopped for any round one or round two, three, four or more.

Port Alexander: Fishing and the Fourth of July

The year 1928 began slowly for the troll fleet at Port Alexander. Salmon prices were low and few king salmon had shown in June as expected. Karl Hansen was the major fish buyer at Port Alexander and was actually the main benefactor for the town also. It was his ingenuity that had a water dam constructed at a small lake across the bay and a water line brought into town to supply everyone. Previously it had been his own packer, *Leif II*, that regularly towed a barge with an immense wooden tank over to Port Conclusion where it was filled with good water at the herring plant located at the head of the bay, then towed back to Port Alexander for public use.

The trollers, dissatisfied with king salmon prices, decided to call a strike in mid-June rather than accept any price less than seventeen cents a pound for mildcure kings with an established break of fourteen pound minimum for mildcure. Karl Hansen, who had contracted to deliver his salmon to Ketchikan Cold Stor-

Port Alexander full of boats in early 1930s.

age, felt unable to meet the demands of the trollers, so things were at an impasse with the Fourth of July only a few days away.

Mass meetings were held nightly by the trollers out on the beach near the entrance to Port Alexander, with a large bonfire to illuminate the speakers, who all voiced their opinions, each one getting more and more inflammatory than the previous speaker, some threatening harm to Karl Hansen if he didn't capitulate and pay the price they demanded.

We kids remained in the background listening to all the threats soon to be inflicted on all fish buyers if they didn't pay the seventeen cents minimum for mildcure salmon. The price had risen to sixteen cents and some of the trollers were anxious to accept it and get busy fishing before any more of the prized salmon swam past on their way south to the Columbia River. However, listening each evening by the bonfire to the threats to be doled out to anyone daring to deliver a salmon for less than seventeen cents, had a very sobering effect and anyone even considering putting a line in the water kept their thoughts to themselves.

A pal, a couple years older than I, who had experience as a troller's crewman at age fourteen, borrowed a rowboat and we rowed outside the harbor to, hopefully, catch a salmon to be divided with our families to eat. I sat in the stern of the skiff while Melvin baited the line, then handed it to me, and commenced rowing toward Breakfast Rock a half mile away.

The baited line had barely straightened out before I felt a tremendous yank on it, that almost tipped me over before I released the line and let it uncoil wildy overboard. Mel had more sense and grabbed the line and put tension on it as it slipped out through his fingers, then rapidly hauled it back as it became slack, and a beautiful large king salmon swam past going in the opposite direction still attached to our line. This madness went on for several more minutes before the king salmon tired enough for Mel to haul it up closely, club it over the head, and haul it into our rowboat where it still crashed around until subdued by more clubbing. What fun and excitement! At the ripe old age of eleven I had never before assisted in catching a troll salmon.

We discussed returning at once with our fish, but Mel, the Captain, decided it would be better to try for another salmon so each of our families would have a complete salmon. This sounded sensible so again we repeated the same procedure with Mel baiting the hook with another herring, and handing the line to me to be paid out again as he rowed forward, letting the line pay out again behind us.

This time it was almost ten minutes before another king salmon struck the bait and I held on wildly until Mel could again take charge and play out another beautiful king salmon that soon lay at our feet beside the first salmon. Now we had our two king salmon but still had four more herring left to be thrown away or utilized as we rowed back to town. We still hadn't reached Breakfast Rock before landing the two kings, and it seemed only sensible to troll at least that far before turning around for home.

The same procedure was again used. Bait the hook, row a short distance, and have another battle with a king salmon before losing the third one which tore loose. This, of course, made us more determined to utilize the remaining three herring, which we did, planning to distribute the extra salmon to friends of the family. One of our catch was a small coho, about five pounds, but still delicious when cooked. Once all the herring were used we rowed towards home. I took over rowing while Mel dressed the salmon on the floor of the boat, a bloody mess, but two proud fishermen could care less. Besides, it was a borrowed skiff.

As we neared the float in the harbor, we had to row past Karl Hansen's fish buying scow, and Mel suggested we stop and inquire if the price had gone up to seventeen cents a pound yet. The workers shook their heads and said, "No." It was still sixteen cents a pound.

We rowed away, but then reconsidered and rowed back to accept sixteen cents a pound for our king salmon. We kept the coho to divide with our families as it was only worth fifty cents altogether. Our four king salmon were worth nearly $16 however, and after Mel took a boat share, Captain's share, and regular share,

Independence Day Port Alexander style

I still received two dollars, and had been initiated into the fishing industry, I thought. Not so, some of the trollers had seen us deliver four king salmon to Karl Hansen's scow at sixteen cents and we were greeted as "SCABS, SCABS, SCABS" all the way as we slunk for home with our coho.

The Fourth of July festivities at Port Alexander were moved up till July first possibly somewhat because two kids had gone right outside the harbor and taken four king salmon and a coho in a couple of hours. Mel and I were both greeted as scabs even by our playmates who had no doubt been indoctrinated at home by their parents to treat us as undesirables. The trollers were confident a settlement was about to be reached momentarily and no one wanted the Fourth of July to interfere, where a few patriotic trollers would remain in town to respect Independence Day while the remainder of the fleet would be rebels and take advantage of less competition.

By noon July first most of the trollers were either drunk or well on their way to getting there. It was Prohibition and liquor was illegal, but moonshine was manufactured locally at twenty dollars a gallon, or good liquor from Prince Rupert, B.C., was also available up at the whorehouses in the lagoon. Their liquor supply was replenished regularly by some of the enterprising halibut boats who delivered their halibut to sell in Prince Rupert and returned to Alaska with a good supply of Scotch selling at twenty dollars a quart, a profit margin of three to four hundred percent. Not bad for an entrepreneur who had herring scales in his eyebrows most of the time.

The dock at Karl Hansen's was cleared and prepared for all the sporting events except the swimming race. This was easily won by Hans Peterson who was a fine athlete. He also overwhelmed all other competition in long jumps, high jumps and hop, skip and jump until it became almost boring to see him awarded one prize after another

When it was time for the pie eating contests, it was difficult for the judges to locate enough participants to enter. In apparent desperation they even accepted Mel and me, the two outcast scabs, to join in the competition. Once we all were down on our knees, with hands behind our backs, it soon became obvious neither Mel or I were going to win any prize even if we devoured our pies in one gulp. The pie eating contest got off to a ragged start with the two scabs getting their pies placed under their face long after the actual race had begun. Anyway, we were both so jubilant even to be allowed to enter, we made no complaint, as it allowed us once again to be part of the group of kids.

The final sporting event was to be held in late afternoon but, before it began, word was passed to the crowd that the Prohis had just arrived by boat and were busily raiding up at the whorehouses and would soon be coming downtown from the lagoon to arrest anyone caught intoxicated or with liquor in their possession. Soon, most of the worst drunks had clambered up on the roof of Karl Hansen's warehouse and, once the despised Prohibition agents came walking down the plank sidewalk, they all began jeering at them and passed their bottles of moonshine back and forth to empty them.

Before the Prohis could actually reach the main crowd, they were met by a delegation of sober citizens who advised them to get their asses back down on their boat and depart as they weren't welcome in Port Alexander. The Prohis must have realized how unpopular they were as they quietly retreated to their boat, untied, and left town.

Now the main event, boxing, was about to begin with, of course, Hans Peterson a heavy favorite to take this event also. He was matched against a Native Indian from Kake who was obviously no match for Hans who had had some professional training. Everyone was back off the roof by now and back beside the ring applauding either for Hans or many for the Native boy who was obviously outclassed.

As the bell rang to complete round one, several scuffles began outside the ring between the rooters for the opposing boxers. By the time round two began inside the ring, all attention was riveted on the fights outside the ring that were more intense and weren't stopped for any round one or round two, three, four or

Karl Hansen's Building (on left) where space out front was roped off for boxing and where drinkers clambered to the roof to get away from prohibition agents during Independence Day celebration.

more. It became necessary to finally separate the fighters outside who by now were all bloody anyway. Oh, yes, the fight inside the ring had also just completed and the judges declared it a draw as most of their attention also had been riveted on the real fighting going on outside.

Down in the harbor earlier in the day, several trollers, each of whom thought he owned the fastest boat in the fleet, had maneuvered up to the starting line in preparation for a quick dash out of the narrow harbor entrance out towards a marker buoy near Breakfast Rock, then back to cross the finish line at the entrance to the harbor. I can't remember how they managed to even get outside the narrow entrance without crashing into each other. I only remember that a boat called *Try Again* won the race.

Next was a tug-of-war between two of the hated herring seiners with Yugoslav crews who spoke only in their own language. They were despised because their taking of massive amounts of herring for the reduction plants nearby was considered to be the major cause of depleted salmon stocks due to lack of herring for their food.

Plus there was resentment that one group of citizens who spoke mostly in their own Yugoslav language could openly make raisin wine by fermenting them in barrels for drinking with their meals aboard their boats, while other citizens were arrested for doing likewise on shore. Adding to the resentment was that many of these herring seiners arrived daily to sell the King salmon they incidently caught in their herring seines to the local fish buyers at prices the trollers were striking to have raised.

The two large herring boats tied a line from each boat and, facing in opposite directions, opened up full power attempting to drag each other over a finish line. Back and forth they drifted with both exhausts smoking, and the crew members shouting in Yugoslav, drowning out any applause on shore. Finally one of the boat's engines overheated and it had to stop and accept defeat amidst the shouting and threats from each boat. And so July first came to an end.

The salmon strike did not end before July fourth, but on July twelfth the order was given to commence trolling at six a.m. The excitement was intense to see if the salmon were still abundant after a month layoff. The first boats in after a full day fishing had only mediocre loads but, when the main fleet began arriving from outside Cape Omaney and Larch Bay, some had tremendous loads of king salmon with *Black Louie* delivering over three hundred dollars worth of kings. There was, however, much complaint about some of the trollers pulling salmon before six a.m.

The only definite eye witness reports were concerning the *Lindy*, a new boat named for Lucky Lindy who had made the non-stop flight to Paris just a year earlier. When the *Lindy* arrived at the float, he was met by a delegation of enraged trollers who insisted he had fished before six a.m., which he insisted had not happened. A rope was brought forth and tied around his neck, and he was marched up the float and onto the dock surrounded by his accusers. A half dozen spectators known as good citizens were selected to be the jury for his hearing and the trial began.

His main accuser, who had loudly been shouting the most, was called forth to make his accusation. However, standing out alone and facing the accused was, apparently, something he hadn't considered. When he was urged to again make his accusation, he was hesitant and when the accused insisted he was mistaken, he became confused and was uncertain if it had been two minutes to six a.m. when he saw a fish taken aboard or ten minutes after six a.m., as the accused insisted had been the correct time he landed his first salmon. He was unable to testify for certain, the accused was untied, and so ended another day at Port Alexander.

YKAH-EEK-QUKA-Sakeen
Goodby
(Thlinget)